An Adirondack Sampler II

An Adirondack Sampler II

Backpacking Trips For All Seasons

BRUCE WADSWORTH

Adirondack Mountain Club, Inc.

Lake George, New York

This book is dedicated to those visionaries of yesteryear whose efforts saw the creation of the Forest Preserve. Because of their wisdom and struggle this magnificent public land exists today for all to use and enjoy.

Published by the Adirondack Mountain Club, Inc.
814 Goggins Road, Lake George, NY 12845-4117
Visit our web site at: **www.adk.org**

Cover and text design: Christopher Kuntze
Cover art: Rachel O'Meara
Photographs by the author unless noted otherwise.

First edition 1981. Reprinted with revisions 1986, 1989, 1992.
Second edition 1995. Reprinted with revisions 1998.

Library of Congress Cataloging-in-Publication Data
Wadsworth, Bruce.
    An Adirondack sampler II : backpacking trips / by Bruce C.
Wadsworth. — 2nd ed.
        p.   cm.
    Includes indexes.
    ISBN 0-935272-75-5 (alk. paper)
        1. Backpacking—New York (State)—Adirondack Mountains—Guidebooks.
    2. Snow camping—New York (State)—Adirondack Mountains—Guidebooks.
    3. Adirondack Mountains (N.Y.)—Guidebooks.
    I. Adirondack Mountain Club. II. Title.
    GV199.42.N652A349   1995
    796.5'1'097475—dc20   95-11687
                                                          CIP

Printed in the United States of America
10 9 8 7 6 5 4 3 2   98 99 00 01 02

Contents

Adirondack Park

1. Pharaoh Lake Wilderness Area
2. Lake George Wild Forest Area
3. Siamese Ponds Wilderness Area
4. Wilcox Lake Wild Forest Area
5. West Canada Lakes Wilderness Area
6. Black River Wild Forest Area
7. Ha-De-Ron-Dah Wilderness Area
8. Pigeon Lake Wilderness Area
9. Santanoni Preserve
10. High Peaks Wilderness Area
11. Five Ponds Wilderness Area
12. Cranberry Lake Wild Forest Area
13. Nehasane

Corrections

Because trail and waterway conditions change, and new boundaries and easements are established, we revise and update our guidebooks regularly. If you come across an error, discrepancy, or need for an update in this guidebook (be sure you are using the latest edition), we want to hear about it so a change can be made in the next edition.

Please address your comments to the publications director of the Adirondack Mountain Club, citing guidebook title, year of edition, section or trail described, page number, and date of your observation. Thanks for your help.

Note: ADK makes every effort to keep its guidebooks up-to-date. However, each printing can only be as current as the last press date; thus, use of this information is at sole risk of the user.

Introduction

An Adirondack Sampler II: Backpacking Trips for All Seasons is a sequel to *An Adirondack Sampler: Day Hikes for All Seasons*. Like the first volume, this book covers a cross-section of the Adirondacks. Even experienced Adirondack hikers often are not familiar with the ninety percent of the Adirondack Park that is outside the High Peaks region. *An Adirondack Sampler II* describes a variety of backpacking trips throughout the Park for the novice and expert alike.

The trail descriptions are primarily two-day outings to accommodate weekend backpackers. In most cases, however, trips can be linked, or suggested options are given so the outings can be extended. These same factors will permit the fast-moving hiker to add items to his or her agenda. References to regional guides are given so the readers can expand their experiences in the areas that might be particularly suited to their tastes and/ or be closer to home.

There are guidebooks for mountain climbers who backpack in order to reach the mountains, and there are guidebooks for backpackers who occasionally climb mountains because they happen to be on the trail being hiked. This book is the latter type. Except for the High Peaks section, the trips described here are not difficult with respect to terrain.

It is the author's belief that a sense of freedom and change from everyday routine are best achieved when time is spent enjoying the country one is passing through rather than on the physical exertion required to reach a destination. The backpacker should commune with, not try to conquer, nature. There should always be time enough to gaze at the scenery, and to think through one's thoughts. This book is for all who seek the camaraderie that comes from a shared wilderness experience, the glow of a campfire, and the sounds of darkness.

The reader should modify the outings described here to match his or her own goals, physical condition, and the experience of each individual member of the backpacking party.

Winter Camping

Many of the trips in this guidebook are well suited to snowshoeing and ski camping. *Inexperienced winter campers should take trips with those trained in winter survival techniques before setting out on their own in winter.* The Adirondack Mountain Club chapters and many other organized groups provide this training. Winter conditions in the Adirondacks can be as severe as any place in the world. Do not take chances.

Carl Heilman II

View from Treadway Mountain

How to Use This Book

Certain methods, expressions, and techniques have been used in this book to convey precise information. This section should be read so that you will understand what these are and why they are used. This will permit you to use the book with greater facility and accuracy.

Trip Headings

DIFFICULTY. Difficulty generally refers to physical problems caused by terrain characteristics. Thus, a long flat hike is not considered difficult, even though it may be tiring. The good day hiker who zips along these trails will feel most of these hikes are easy. The overnight backpacker carrying 30 or 40 pounds of gear may consider the same trips much more difficult.

TRIP DISTANCE. Novices sometimes get in over their heads because they think only in terms of how far it is to a given destination, forgetting that an equal distance must be traveled on the return trip. Saying a trip is five miles to a given destination conveys something rather different from saying it is a 10-mile round-trip hike. Because loop trips often have different return distances from the outgoing section, it is often misleading to simply assume doubling the one-way distance will be accurate. In this guide, the heading at the beginning of each trip description will use Round-Trip Distance for loop trips and will state Through-Trip Distance for through trips.

TIME NECESSARY. The time given is that which most people seeking a relaxing trip will take. A day hiker could complete many of these trips in a single day, but the backpacker may choose to stay three days at a lake two miles from the trailhead before completing the trip. These are factors you must work out for yourself.

MAPS. Maps are simply symbols placed on a sheet of paper in a usable configuration to help you find your way. Symbols must be interpreted. The user of maps must compare the symbols on the map with the terrain being traveled and then make necessary judgements as to how to proceed.

For example, it is important to be alert for barrier symbols on maps. Barriers separating private land from state land generally restrict passage by the hiker, while barriers at the beginning of state trails generally restrict passage by vehicles. The symbol for a woods road does not mean use of vehicles is necessarily permitted. In Forest Preserve areas designated wilderness, unauthorized vehicular use is never permitted. Therefore the symbol for a woods road simply means a dirt road of some sort exists- an old tote road, a carriage lane from the past, or perhaps an abandoned jeep trail. They can generally be considered likely possibilities for

cross-country skiing, but never assume they authorize motorized travel.
Below is a legend, showing symbols commonly used on the maps
found in this book.

Legend

Topographic maps are usually called quadrangles. Two long-term
changes with maps, now occurring, can cause confusion and require
careful attention when selecting maps. The first change concerns the
series available and the second change involves the units of measure-
ment used.

Series. The ground represented on a topographic map is the area of earth
surface within a specific range of latitude and longitude. Since a map of
your town park and a map of the United States could each be printed on
the same size paper, it is necessary to have a way to let the user know
how much land is really represented on a particular map. The term for
this information is the series of the map. It is expressed in angle degrees
of latitude and longitude.

There are 360 angle degrees in the circle that encompasses the Earth.
However, a map representing only one degree of latitude by one degree
of longitude of the whole Earth's ground surface would be a map that
could show about one-fourth of the Adirondack Park. The hiker would
either have a map far too large to carry around in a pack or a map so
small in scale that none of the detailed ground information needed
could be shown on the map. In order to show the needed detail on a
reasonable size piece of paper in print large enough to read, only a relatively small amount of ground surface can be represented on a topographic map. This means that the angle degree must be divided into
smaller units in much the way yards are broken into inches if you
need smaller units.

Thus, one degree can be divided into 60 minutes and one minute of angle can be further subdivided into 60 seconds. Remember, these are angle minutes and seconds, not time minutes and seconds. The abbreviations for these units are ' for minutes and " for seconds.

Until about 20 years ago almost all Adirondack maps were 15-minute series maps, showing an area 1/4-degree latitude x 1/4-degree longitude. (Think that one through. Remember, there are 60 minutes in a degree.) In a region like the Mount Marcy area of the High Peaks, where there are many trails in a small area, more detail was needed. So 7.5-minute series maps were produced. These showed only one-quarter of the ground surface of the 15-minute series map but were on slightly bigger pieces of paper and could thus show far greater detail.

Then came the change of topographic maps to the metric system. This arrived just in time for the 1980 Olympics and the Lake Placid area was the first place in the country to have the new maps. Metric topographic maps are now standard; this is what you usually will find in stores if you buy a new map for the Adirondacks today. These are 7.5-minute x 15-minute series maps. This means each map shows a ground area of 7.5 minutes latitude (tall) x 15 minutes longitude (wide). It's like having half a 15-minute series map or placing two 7.5-minute series maps side by side. It shows great detail since it is on a rather large size piece of paper.

Be careful that the map you are purchasing shows the desired area: different series maps having the same map name actually show different ground areas. Look before buying!

Units. Most young hikers have grown up with the metric system, have used it daily in science classes and are quite comfortable with it. Many hikers of "longer experience," however, finished their school years without metrics and find the new maps a bit confusing. Contour intervals on metric maps are in meters, not feet. Instead of the usual 20-foot contour interval, most metric maps you will use will have a 10-meter contour interval. This is approximately 33 feet. In practical terms, contour lines appear farther apart on the map. For a hiker conditioned to 20-foot contours, it may seem that terrain being climbed is a lot steeper than the metric map contours make it appear to you. Frequent use of metric maps will quickly reorient your mind.

On the positive side, the larger scale of the map compared to the 15-minute series maps usually means the print is larger and the symbols farther apart. This makes reading the map easier. If unfamiliar with using kilometers, you can usually avoid potential problems by converting distances to miles on the distance scales found at the bottom of the maps.

To help you through the transitional stages of "going metric," both English and metric measuring units are used in this book. You will find that if you use just the metric units rather than trying to convert from one unit to the other, you'll soon have no difficulty.

Standard Abbreviations

mi. = mile
km = kilometer(s)
yd(s) = yard(s)
m = meter(s)
ft. = foot, feet
cm = centimeter(s)
in. = inch(es)
39.4 inches = 1 meter
1000 meters = 1 kilometer
1 kilometer = 0.6 miles
1 mile = 1.62 kilometers

Directional Guidelines

1. As is standard practice, the right and left sides of a stream are determined as the observer faces downstream. Thus, if you are walking upstream on the right side of a southward flowing stream, you would be on the west bank of the stream.
2. Since you will be referring directly to your compass while hiking, magnetic compass readings have been given in the text.

   If you take map angles to determine direction and intend to use a compass from those map angles, you must account for magnetic declination, which is approximately 14 degrees west in the Adirondacks. Converting map angles to compass angles must be done accurately to prevent your becoming lost in the woods. If you do not possess this skill, get a good book and study up on compass use before heading for the trail.

Land Classification

The Adirondack Park is approximately the size of the state of Connecticut. This is larger than the combined sizes of Yellowstone, Yosemite, and Glacier national parks. Yet, if you asked a hiker where he went for the weekend, he is likely simply to say, "to the Adirondacks."

To encourage a better understanding of the Adirondack Park, the names of different areas as stated in the *Adirondack Park State Land Master Plan* have been used in this book.

The great majority of the publicly owned part of the Adirondack Park, i.e. the Forest Preserve, is divided into one of three land classifications: Wilderness, Wild Forest, and Primitive areas. Parts of the definitions of these three land classifications as found in the *Adirondack Park State Land Master Plan* follow.

The most wild and natural part of the Forest Preserve is the Wilderness Area: "Wilderness Area, in contrast with those areas where man and his own works dominate the landscape, is an area where the earth and its community of life are untrammeled by man ... where man himself is a visitor who does not remain." Wilderness areas are usually 10,000 acres or larger in size. There are currently 16 Wilderness areas in the Adirondack Park.

In contrast, "A Wild Forest Area is an area where the resources permit a somewhat higher degree of human use than in Wilderness, Primitive, or Canoe areas, while retaining an essentially wild character." One major difference between the two areas is that motorized vehicles are not permitted in Wilderness areas, whereas they are permitted into Wild Forest areas under certain conditions. There are 17 Wild Forest areas in the Adirondack Park.

Primitive areas are lands whose characteristics fall somewhere between those of the Wilderness and Wild Forest areas. A truly wild land area may be classified as Primitive if it is small and so affected by private land around it that it can never develop a wilderness character. Most Primitive areas, however, are in a state of transition. Human use prior to becoming part of the Forest Preserve resulted in loss of wilderness characteristics. These characteristics will return in time, and it is anticipated that these areas will eventually be reclassified as Wilderness areas. There are 24 Primitive areas in the Adirondack Park.

Changes in Grade

The terms gradual, moderate, moderately steep, steep and very steep appear throughout the book to suggest change in vertical grade. How "steep" a grade is to the hiker depends on physical condition, whether the grade occurs at the beginning or the end of the trip, the size of the backpack, whether the trail is icy and many other factors. The actual steepness of a particular slope doesn't change, but the hiker's mental attitude toward it does, depending on the resultant of these forces.

Considerable care was taken in the use of these terms, so that steep in one trail description matched what was meant by steep as used in all the other trail descriptions. The hiker using this guide may think that moderate as used in the guide is really steep. That happens when descriptive terms are used by different people. It is hoped that the hiker, after using a few trail descriptions in this book, will be able to reconcile the author's meaning with his/her own concept and use this adjustment for mentally getting a true picture of other hikes described in the book.

Glossary

Bushwhack
To make one's way through bushes or undergrowth.

Cairn
A pile of rocks or stones to mark a summit or route.

Gradual

Moderate

Moderately steep

Steep

Very steep

Steepness Standards

Campsites
(a) Informal: A campsite without structures, other than a fire ring. It may or may not conform to DEC regulations or the State Land Master Plan of the region.
(b) Designated: A campsite marked with a sign (a teepee symbol) indicating a legal campsite in an otherwise nonconforming location.
(c) No Camping: An old campsite no longer legally usable due to its nonconforming location. Marked with a sign (a teepee with an X through it).

Col
The highest point of a pass across a ridge between two adjacent peaks.

Contour
An imaginary plane of unchanging elevation.

Corduroy
A road, trail, or bridge formed by logs laid side by side transversely to facilitate crossing swampy places.

Duff
Partly decayed vegetable matter on a forest floor.

Fork
A place where one route divides into two routes.

Hardwoods
Broad-leaf deciduous trees.

Lean-to
An open camp with overhanging roof on the open side.

Logging Road
A road used for removing logs from the forest. Many present-day hiking trails are on former logging roads.

Massif
A large rocky prominence.

Mixed Wood
A forest composed of both broad-leaf deciduous trees and cone-bearing coniferous trees.

Outcrop
A place where the bedrock of an area breaks the surface of the ground.

Paint Blazes
A blaze is where the bark of the tree has been cut to leave a scar. The scar is then painted to make an easily seen trail marker.

Softwoods
Cone-bearing coniferous trees.

Stillwater
A section of river where either natural or manmade barriers back up the water a long distance. Free flow of the stream is thus prevented.

Switchback
A sharp turn in the trail, made so that a generally desired direction can be maintained and at the same time the rate of incline of the trail can be kept moderate. Switchbacks occur in series on steep sections of trail.

Terrain
The surrounding land surface.

Topography
The degree of variation found in the terrain's elevation.

Vlei (vly)
An old Dutch term for a marshy or swampy area.

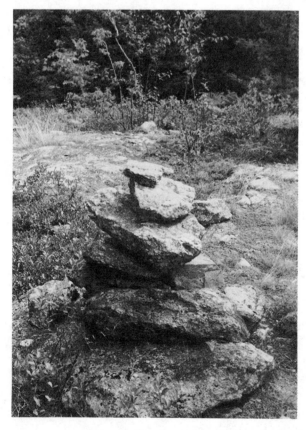

A cairn

Trail Habits and Practices

The Adirondack Park consists of privately owned lands interspersed with the publicly owned Forest Preserve. Often the access trails to state-owned land cross private property. They are kept open due to the courtesy and thoughtfulness of the landowners. It is important that the users of these private lands show the same courtesy and thoughtfulness by their actions and conduct.

The Forest Preserve is for all to use and enjoy. Sound forest practices will help sustain and improve the quality of both the land and the experience enjoyed by the backpacker.

Good trail manners make good friends. Good camping practices preserve the forest so that the next user will be able to enjoy it to its fullest extent. In addition, there are DEC regulations which must be followed. Some of the most basic of these manners, practices, and regulations are presented on the following pages. Woodswise campers know them to be sound. Beginners should adopt them.

Users should consider themselves stewards of the land for future generations. It is not enough to love nature; it is necessary to carry out actions that will sustain and improve this great land.

On the Trail

1. For safety, hike in groups of four or more. Keep the group together. In case of injury, send more than one person for help to be sure the word gets through.
2. Be sure someone at home knows the specific part of the Adirondacks where you are hiking and your intended return time. Always sign in and out at trail registers.
3. Watch for trail markers. Know the general lay of the land you are traveling. Have both map and compass and know how to use them.

Selecting Campsites

1. Camping, except at designated sites, is not permitted within 150 ft. of roads, trails, springs, streams, ponds, and other bodies of water (DEC reg.).
2. Camp on high ground and away from water to find a favorable breeze and avoid bugs.
3. Lean-tos cannot be reserved. They are available to all campers on a first come basis until capacity of the lean-to has been reached (DEC reg.).
4. It is wise to select a suitable camp early enough to get set up before dark. Keep a weather eye out to avoid having to make camp in the rain.

In Camp

1. Fires can be built only for cooking, warmth, or smudge (DEC reg.). Be careful if using tobacco products products (field strip, burn or carry out butts).
2. It is illegal to cut live wood on state lands (NYS law). Cut only dead and down wood.
3. Use established privies whenever possible. If such privies are not available, make a slit trench well away from camp and from water. Be sure to cover human waste with soil and leaves. Burn toilet paper in winter.
4. Do not wash yourself, clothes, or dishes in a natural body of water. Use a container to collect water and use it away from the source. Use only biodegradable soaps and detergents. Dispose of waste well away from the source of water.
5. You'll be more comfortable and have less difficulty with pests and animals if you keep food away from sleeping areas.
6. Hang food well away from the camping area, at least 15 feet up in the air and well extended from the reach of tree-climbing bears. Do not leave snacks in your pack unless you want chipmunks and squirrels in your pack.
7. Set up tents in level or slightly rounded areas. Avoid low spots where rainwater will collect. It is not considered good practice to ditch tents.
8. Do not litter. Burn all burnables and remember that aluminum packages will not burn. Carry out all nonburnables.
9. Leave your campsite cleaner than you found it. It is an old custom to leave dry firewood for the next camper.
10. Do not leave boots or other items out where porcupines can carry them off.
11. No group of 10 or more campers can camp on State Lands at any time except under permit (DEC reg.). Permits are available from the forest ranger in whose area you are camping.
12. Temporary camping in one location for more than three nights is prohibited except under permit (DEC reg.).
13. Use suitable filter or water purifier to insure against Giardia—especially in heavily used areas. Chemical purifiers are better. Get drinking water upstream from your campsite.

On the Way Out

1. If you carried it in full, you can certainly carry it out empty. Do not litter the forests. A good woodsperson will leave a campsite in better condition than he or she found it. Take a litter bag along in your pack.
2. Mark OUT beside your name on the trail register, so others know you have returned.
3. Share your knowledge of problem areas or campsites with others you meet on the trail.

If Lost

1. Sit down in one place for at least 15 minutes to collect your senses. A simple overlooked fact that can unravel the problem will often come to mind.
2. If you are convinced you are really lost, find an open spot where aircraft can spot you. A nearby high land area may provide sightings that can be matched with your map to provide needed information. Do not wander aimlessly.
3. Pick a good place to stay. You will be found if you have let someone at home know where you are going and have given instructions for what to do if you are not home by a given time.

The Adirondack Mountain Club has several pamphlets of interest to the backpacker: Backcountry Tips for the Backpacker (English and French); Backwoods Sanitation and Giardia (English and French); For the Winter Hiker and Backcountry Skier (English); Hypothermia and Frostbite; Taking a Hike, Leading a Hike; and Hiking with Children. These may be obtained for a small charge by writing the Adirondack Mountain Club, Inc., 814 Goggins Road, Lake George, New York 12845-4117.

Tips on Bear-Proofing Your Campsite

* Never store food in your tent.
* Wrap odiferous foods well.
* Wrap trash in sealed plastic bags or other sealed containers.
* Hang clothes worn while cooking with your pack. They hold food odors and attract bears.
* Keep a clean fire pit. Grease and food scraps will attract bears.
* Hang packs from a high branch incapable of holding a bear's weight.
* Report any bear encounters to the nearest forest ranger or ranger station.

Equipment and Vittles

The specific equipment you carry and the kinds of food you consume depend on many factors. How long will you be on the trail? What will you be doing? Is your budget large or small? How strong are you? Are you in good physical condition? Do you wish to rough it or smooth it? How many times a year do you use your gear?

Before making a significant investment, do some serious thinking about your real needs. Generally, five factors should be considered: comfort, adaptability to changing conditions, health, safety, and your personal interests. Rate any intended purchase against these five criteria.

Serviceability will soon take precedence over such things as fancy laces, pretty decals, or color. Buy the best you can afford, but remember that no matter what the quality, you'll never enjoy using the equipment if it doesn't fit you well or if you don't feel comfortable with it.

Assimilate all the information you can from any and all sources, but base the final decisions upon your own assessment of how well the items meet the parameters you yourself have established.

Equipment

Following is a general listing of gear and things to consider when choosing equipment.

SUGGESTED PERSONAL EQUIPMENT

map, compass and guidebook

Gear

suitable pack, tent with waterproof fly, ground cloth, sleeping bag with waterproof stuff bag, sleeping pad, rain gear (for you and for pack), water bottle/canteen, small/medium sized lock blade or fixed blade knife, flashlight (with extra batteries and bulb), nested cooking gear, plate or large bowl, eating utensils, can opener, cooking stove, cleaning pads, stove fuel, food

Clothing

hats (one wool, one soft with brim), mosquito head net and insect repellent in season, good hiking boots, extra shoes (moccasins or sneakers), several pair of socks, jacket or sweater, long sleeved shirt, long trousers, shorts and/or swim suit, large handkerchiefs, extra underwear, mittens

Toilet articles

washcloth and towel, toothbrush, toothpaste, comb, hair brush, cream or lotion, biodegradable soap, toilet tissue, sanitary items, nail file and clippers

Emergency materials

long burning candle and extra matches, solar blanket, whistle, sewing kit, safety pins, small coil wire, pencil and paper, steel mirror, several plastic bags (assorted sizes), repair kit for tent and gear, small pair of pliers, waterproof tape

Suggested common equipment

water purification chemicals or water filters, collapsible bucket/bag, bear bag line (60 ft.) plus 50 ft. extra ⅛" nylon rope

First aid kit

first aid manual, sterile gauze, adhesive tape, triple ointment, percogesic pills, zinc ointment, bee sting allergy treatment chemicals, 1 oz. green soap, band-aids, one 6-inch bandage, aspirin, second skin or mole skin patches, milk of magnesia tablets, special medications as needed, one ace bandage, scissors, tweezers

Optional materials

daily log book, camera, fishing gear, books, playing cards, ditty bags for personal items, binoculars, hiking stick

THINGS TO CONSIDER ABOUT EQUIPMENT

Sleeping bags

1. Synthetic materials are often preferable in the damp eastern United States; down loses its insulation properties when wet.
2. Liners prolong the life of your sleeping bag and keep it clean.
3. Double bags can be used year-round.

Packs

1. External frames or internal suspension frames are needed for backpacking.
2. A hip pad greatly increases personal comfort.
3. A pack must be large enough for the job and must fit well.

Tent

1. A tent is a necessity. You cannot rely on having an empty lean-to.
2. Weight is important, but so is the amount of room needed. Will your gear fit into the tent if it rains?

Boots

1. Boots are your most important equipment.
2. Boots must fit properly; break them in before taking a long hike with pack.
3. Medium-weight boots are needed when a heavy pack is used. Avoid heavyweight boots designed for climbing Anapurna unless you are climbing Anapurna.

4. Moccasins feel awfully good around camp after a long day on the trail. Having an alternate set of footwear also allows your boots to dry out at night.

Cooking Gear

1. Carry a camp stove. Frequently used campsites will not have adequate firewood.
2. Consider the type of stove needed. Some fuels don't light easily in frigid weather. Will you need to melt a lot of snow for water? How many people will you be cooking for?
3. Consider the nesting cook kits. Stainless steel cookware, rather than aluminum, is recommended for camping.

First-Aid Kit

1. Carry a good one and know how to use it.
2. Extended wilderness trips require extra supplies of Band-Aids and perhaps an inflatable splint. One good complete kit per party is more useful than several individual kits.

Flashlight

1. The first time a porcupine is chewing at your sleeping bag in the dark you'll know why you need one.
2. Purchase one good one or you'll be forever buying cheap ones.
3. You can't carry a candle to the privy in a rain storm.

Rain Gear

1. A poncho should be large enough to cover both you and your pack.
2. If you prefer a rain jacket and rain chaps to a poncho, have a separate cover for your pack. A large plastic garbage bag can be used in an emergency.

Finally, the equipment won't do you any good unless you take it with you. Make a list of the equipment you want to take, or simply refer to the list in this book. Then check off the items as you pack.

In Transit

Some thought should be given to carrying your equipment in your vehicle from home to trailhead. Be sure your fuel can is safe and doesn't leak. Be careful that the upright canteen in your pack doesn't leak when you lay the pack on its side in the car trunk. Don't store your camera film in a hot car trunk.

When you start hiking, put your wallet, car keys, important papers, etc. in a small ditty bag. Then put the ditty bag in your pack. It's more comfortable to hike with empty pockets, and you won't lose the items on the trail or through a crack in the lean-to floor.

Vittles

The food you consume on camping trips should be nourishing and somewhat higher than normal in energy. There is, however, a vast difference between what the backpacker out for the weekend and the backpacker on the Northville–Placid Trail for two weeks needs to consider.

First of all, consider the total weight of food you can carry. The long-trip hiker has perhaps 20 meals to tote along. Weight is a factor. Dehydrated food (expensive) and freeze-dried food (very expensive) may well be needed to reduce the bulk and weight. On the other hand, the weekend camper probably has three meals to lug along. Weight won't be all that important, and under these circumstances practically anything can be carried.

The pancake mix in the supermarket is the same as the pancake mix in the camping store, so don't pay fancy prices for camping food even though you are going out for a week or more. In fact, granola, cool drink mixes, spaghetti, noodles, rice, dried meat, and numerous other foods are readily available in most food stores at a fraction of the cost camping stores will charge.

The weekend camper should consider what utensils are needed. Freeze-dried foods may only require adding hot water to the packages they come in, and if what you really want is a lazy weekend in the sun, or if you want shrimp cocktails, hollandaise sauce, and beef stroganoff without any mess or fuss, it may be worth your while to spend the extra money on camp food.

The point is that specially prepared camping food is a luxury, not a necessity, for backpacking.

The backpacker who uses nothing but dehydrated or freeze-dried food for extensive lengths of time may have another type of problem. The food is so concentrated and its roughage so reduced that normal bodily activities are prevented and the camper becomes constipated. Thus, it is wise to have a certain amount of fresh food in your diet. Stewed prunes may not be your choice for breakfast fruit, but many campers on long trips wish they had some.

Some backpackers prefer to have solid breakfast and end-of-day meals but no large time-consuming mid-day meals. Instead, they pack cheese, gorp, candy, and cookies. Then, whenever a rest break is taken during the day, they nibble and munch. This prevents that overstuffed feeling while hiking and insures a steady supply of nutrients all day long.

One last thing. Many people don't realize that water is a nutrient. See how long you can go without it! Trip planning should include knowing what water sources are along your route of travel. If the available supply is in doubt, carry a full water bottle. Drink it freely at regular intervals. It is more important to you than food, since you probably have a little fat to give you energy. If there are many streams and ponds along your hiking route, it may save quite a bit of weight to carry a filter instead of a great deal of water. Drink and refilter along the way. (Remember, however, that most filters do not eliminate viruses.) Purification of water by chemical methods is also practical for a few days, but generally is not recommended for long time periods—occasionally thyroid problems develop owing to too much iodine.

Emergency Procedures

Emergencies aren't planned; they just happen. You should be prepared to handle minor emergencies.

If assistance is needed you should know how to go about obtaining it. First, mark on a map the location where the emergency exists and take the map with you for reference by those you contact for help. If the emergency involves an injury, write down the condition of the patient and the time you left for help. Be sure you have vehicle keys with you if you intend to drive for help from the trailhead. If the party is large enough, send more than one person out to get help. (If only one goes and that person is disabled enroute, you have two emergencies and no one to get help.)

If there is a trail register enroute, check it. Often, local telephone numbers to call for aid and other local specific emergency information is provided for hikers.

When you reach a telephone, call any emergency number you found listed at trail registers or call (518) 891-0235. That number will get you to the DEC Region 5 emergency personnel in Ray Brook, New York, or will automatically transfer you to a New York State police unit. Most of the trips in this book are in Region 5. Region 6 area emergencies will be transferred to the correct people.

1. The Pharaoh Lake Wilderness Area

Pharaoh Lake Wilderness Area has perhaps the best network of foot trails in the Adirondack Park outside of the High Peaks. Over 46,000 acres, plus the adjoining Crane Pond and Bald Ledge primitive areas, provide a combined total of 44.6 mi. (72.3 km) of foot trails.

There are 35 bodies of water in the Pharaoh Lake Wilderness Area and four more in the Crane Pond Primitive Area. Fifteen lean-tos are found in this region. Several of the ponds have been reclaimed and now have excellent trout fishing.

Pharaoh Mountain with its 2556 ft. (782 m) elevation is the highest peak in the region. Treadway Mt. is also a very rewarding peak to climb. Many of the peaks and knobs of this section have bare rock summits that invite bushwhack trips into trailless areas. Though the mountain tops have relatively low elevations, the vertical ascent from base to summit is often considerable, since the base elevation of the whole region is also low. This is often overlooked by climbers who note only summit elevations and draw the erroneous conclusion that the only challenging climbs to be found are in the High Peaks.

The trips described here are reasonably short overnighters, but they can be linked to make a good week's outing. Actually, you could probably spend two or more weeks in this area and seldom retrace your steps. For instance, you might go from Rock Pond to Clear Pond to Grizzle Ocean, then back to Putnam Pond to make a three-day outing. On a week's trip you could extend from Grizzle Ocean to Pharaoh Lake, over Pharaoh Mountain to Crane Pond, then back to Rock Pond via Crab and Horseshoe ponds. For more information about this region, see *Guide to Adirondack Trails: Eastern Region* (ADK).

Bear Pond—Rock Pond Loop and Options

Difficulty: Generally easy
Round Trip Distance: 6.0 mi. (9.7 km)
Time Necessary: 2 days
Map: Paradox Lake 15' Series

The trip goes from pond to pond in a leisurely fashion over excellent trails. It can easily be lengthened by visiting still more ponds or by bushwhacking a peak or two, and there are other possible trips if you really want to cover more ground. This outing is especially for the hiker who likes to study the fauna and flora, snap a few pictures, and maybe take a long afternoon swim. With full pack the trip will seem longer than it would appear to be on a map. Once in awhile it's nice just to take it easy and do a little fishing.

Trailhead access is from Putnam Pond Public Campground and Day Use Area. It is reached off Rte. 74 from Ticonderoga in the east and from Exit 28 of the Adirondack Northway in the west. Turn off Rte. 74 at Chilson, where a large Putnam Pond Public Campground sign is seen. It is 3.8 mi. (6.2 km) to the toll gate at the campground. Bear right from the toll gate and, after crossing a bridge in a road dip, take the second lefthand turn. This takes you to the day-use area, where your vehicle can be left in a large parking lot.

Returning on foot to the road you turned from, turn left again and walk about 0.3 mi. (0.5 km). If you stay on the main road, you'll wind up around a grade and arrive at the trailhead, near Campsite #38. A signpost is located here.

DAY 1. The trail drops down a grade from the signpost (0.0 mi.), curving northward beside the outlet of Heart Pond. Walking almost on the level, yellow DEC trail markers take you 0.3 mi. (0.5 km) to a junction within sight of Heart Pond.

The trail to the left leads to Rock Pond. Your route turns to the right, crossing the muddy outlet of Heart Pond on logs. The blue-marked trail is noticeably less used than the trail on the earlier part of the hike. You swing past Heart Pond and continue northward through a splendid hardwood forest. Numerous white birches stand out in this section. The almost imperceptible grade and leaf-covered trail make walking very enjoyable. Large hemlocks are occasionally seen, and at one point the trail crosses a base rock area. Here the woods open up and blueberries abound in season.

A T-junction appears at 1.4 mi. (2.4 km). The unmarked route to the right follows an old lumber road several miles to Chilson. Turn left and walk another 0.1 mi. (0.2 km). An unmarked path to the right leads over a knoll to the shore of Bear Pond. This pretty body of water has no obvious camp sites, but there are several spots that would be ideal.

Beyond the unmarked path, the trail reaches the southern end of Bear Pond in about 40 yds. (37 m). This part of the pond isn't nearly so attractive as that seen by taking the aforementioned path.

Turning abruptly left, the trail follows the edge of the pond, crosses its outlet on logs, and proceeds along the south shore. It then veers to the northwest briefly before resuming a southwesterly course with a long moderate climb up an old switchbacking tote road. At about 2.2 mi. (3.6 km), the 350 ft. (109 m) ascent brings you to a col having an approximate elevation of 1750 ft. (535 m).

An equally long grade takes you down to Rock Pond. The whole route from Bear Pond to Rock Pond is most interesting. At 2.9 mi. (4.7 km) the wide trail both narrows and steepens. Soon after crossing an open rock slide zone, you arrive at the shoreline of Rock Pond. A trail junction can be missed here if you are not careful. A red-marked trail circles the pond to the right. (From this junction, there are several options, depending on the interest of the hiker. The options are listed below, but regardless of the op-

Pharaoh Lake Wilderness Area

tion selected, the hiker is encouraged to visit the iron mine site described in option 1.)

Option 1 – Turn right (west) and follow the red marked trail counterclockwise around Rock Pond.

Option 2 – Turn left (east), walk a short distance to a junction; turn right again and walk a short distance to the Rock Pond lean-to.

Option 3 – Follow Option 2, but continue beyond the lean-to, following guidebook map to Clear Pond lean-to.

Option 1 includes the iron mine visit and is described here. The route swings to the right, following the red-marked trail. Almost immediately a large iron cylinder is seen to the right; then old stone foundations whet your curiosity. Another 50 yds. (47 m) brings you to a fascinating old iron mine cutting into solid rock, and a side trail leads uphill past the mine a short way to the remains of a flooded open-pit mine . These are two of the many abandoned mines which were operated during the Civil War and post-Civil War eras. The runoff carries a reddish iron material into Rock Pond, but it doesn't seem to affect its aquatic life, which is flourishing.

Continuing beyond the mine, along the red marked trail, at 3.2 mi. (5.2 km), there are approximately 200 yds. (183 m) of somewhat hazardous trail. Here, a very steep rock wall requires you to sidle up a narrow trail; a hiker with full pack must be careful to maintain balance. It is not recommended if it is wet. However, the section is so short and what is beyond it so nice that there is every reason to continue along this route, with suitable caution, in good weather.

Once past this point, the going is easier and you soon reach the great open rock formation that gives the pond its name. Rising out of the water, this massif makes an ideal place for a cooling swim and lunch break. (In fact, there are several rough fireplaces found here. It would be an ideal camping spot.) Between this point and the two lean-tos on the opposite side of the pond, you will find several more excellent campsites. The pond trail circles to the north and becomes a very pleasant level route, staying close to the water.

At 3.7 mi. (6.0 km) the Lilypad Pond trail comes in from the right. This trail leads 1.1 mi. (l.8 km) to Lilypad Pond, where a lean-to is located. From there, the trail branches left for Horseshoe Pond and right for Arnold Pond.

The Rock Pond Trail continues southeast to the 3.9 mi. (6.3 km) point, where another junction is reached. Here, the Clear Pond trail enters from the right at an acute angle. It is 1.1 mi. (1.8 km) to Clear Pond, which has a lean-to on its eastern shoreline. Clear Pond has a trail around it, from which a trail to North Pond and another to Grizzle Ocean and Putnam Pond branch off.

The Rock Pond trail soon reaches the neck between Rock Pond and Little Rock Pond. This is crossed on a wooden bridge and brings you to another junction. The yellow-marked trail to the right leads 0.1 mi. (0.2 km) to the

Little Rock Pond lean-to. This lean-to is in excellent shape but is hidden in the trees, pointing away from the water. One wonders why the almost perfect location for a shelter just before the lean-to was overlooked.

The pond trail now follows yellow markers north of this junction. At 4.2 mi. (6.8 km) the Rock Pond lean-to is reached. It sits surrounded by large trees, back a short distance from the shoreline.

From here it is only 0.1 mi. (0.2 km) to another junction. A very short distance around the pond from this junction will bring you to the Bear Pond trail junction mentioned at about 3.0 mi. (4.9 km).

A right turn at this junction leads to North Pond.

DAY 2. It is assumed you camped somewhere around Rock Pond on Day 1. A long hike can return you to Putnam Pond Campground via Clear Pond and the eastern shore of Putnam Pond.

The described route is a much shorter trip. Beginning at the junction 0.1 mi. (0.2 km) northeast of the Rock Pond lean-to, turn right and proceed towards North Pond. At 4.5 mi. (7.3 km), a junction is reached. Here, a yellow trail leads to Little Rock Pond and then to Clear Pond.

Continue straight ahead for North Pond. Heading south, it is only 0.3 mi. (0.5 km) to the trailhead at Putnam Pond at Putnam Pond Public Campground. A short, moderate grade takes you over a ridge, and a longer moderate grade takes you down to a junction within sight of North Pond at 5.0 mi. (8.1 km). North Pond was once distinct from Putnam Pond, connected by a narrow channel through a marshy area. Construction of the dam at the Putnam Pond outlet raised the water level. Modern maps make North Pond seem to be only a lobe of Putnam Pond.

A sharp left at this junction takes you through a series of short, moderately steep ups and downs. At 5.6 mi. (9.1 km) an unmarked path to the left, just before a steep dip, guides you out to a high peninsula jutting out into Heart Pond. This beautiful little spot is a good place for a short photographic break.

The Bear Pond junction is reached at 5.7 mi. (9.2 km). It is only 0.3 mi. (0.5 km) straight ahead to the trailhead at Putnam Pond Public Campground.

Grizzle Ocean and Treadway Mountain

Difficulty: Easy trail, easy mountain
Round Trip Distance: 7.4 mi. (12.0 km)
Time Necessary: 2 days
Map: Paradox Lake 15' Series

This can be an extremely easy beginner's outing into Grizzle Ocean for a total 3.8 mi. (6.2 km) round trip if Treadway Mountain is skipped. However, Treadway Mountain should not be skipped. It is a remarkably easy mountain to climb, even with full pack. Offering a full-circle vista from its bare, solid quartz summit, you'll spend a long time gazing out at the surrounding lakes, ponds, and forest before leaving it. The descent will get you over to Grizzle Ocean for a refreshing swim before supper. It's not very big, and there's no salt air breeze, but it's the only "ocean" we've got in the Adirondacks.

Access to the trailhead is from the toll booth at the Putnam Pond Public Campsite and Day Use Area. Refer to the Bear Pond–Rock Pond Loop trip and use the same directions for arriving at the campsite.

From the toll booth, take the left side of the fork in front of you. Drive along Putnam Creek to Putnam Pond. Continue past the boat launching site, at 0.2 mi. (0. 3 km). Soon after swinging around a bend to the left, you will see trailhead signs. A large parking area is on the right, just beyond the trail signs. (Do not mistakenly take the Berrymill Pond trail, which begins at the far end of the parking area.)

The trail begins at the DEC trail signs (0.0 mi.) at the west end of the parking area. Follow yellow trail markers over minor ups and downs that will soon level out as you walk along the east shore of Putnam Pond. An unmarked trail forks right, five minutes down the trail. It leads 0.1 mi. (0.2 km) to a picnic table on the shore of Putnam Pond.

Bearing left from the fork, the route moves back from the pond. Before long, you begin a gradual upgrade. The way becomes quite rocky, developing a moderate grade through a splendid grove of hemlocks. Height of land is soon reached at 0.7 mi. (1.1 km), where a moderately steep descent continues through hemlocks.

A split log bridge takes you over the large outlet of Berrymill Pond. Five minutes later, a trail junction with signs is reached. This is the 1.2 mi. (1.9 km) point. Here the side trail leads 0.1 mi. (0.2 km) to the right to a boat landing.

Continuing straight ahead for another 10 minutes brings you to a second split log bridge. Crossing over the outlet of Grizzle Ocean, another trail junction is immediately seen, at 1.4 mi. (2.3 km). The yellow trail straight ahead leads 0.5 mi. (0.8 km) to Grizzle Ocean. The continuing trail description takes you up Treadway Mountain before heading for Grizzle Ocean from this junction. This stream is the last sure water on the summit trail.

Turn right and follow the blue-marked Clear Pond trail toward Treadway Mountain. Rolling terrain is easily traveled as you skirt a small vlei. A four-way trail junction is reached at 1.8 mi. (2.9 km). The trail straight ahead continues another 0.4 mi. (0.6 km) to Clear Pond, which has a lean-to. The trail right leads 0.2 mi. (0.3 km) to a boat landing on Putnam Pond. (Snowshoers ascend Treadway in winter by walking the Putnam Pond ice to this boat landing.)

Turn left and follow red trail markers. A short, moderate slope soon levels. Comfortable trail takes you around the south edge of a beaver bog near Mud Pond. A rocky outcrop is passed. The trail turns left after crossing a brook on a log bridge. Level trail becomes a gradual upgrade and then briefly a moderate grade before again leveling off. The mixed wood forest has some large beech and maple. The hiker with a full pack should have little difficulty.

You continue up varying grades with intervening level stretches where you can catch your breath. A bare rock slide zone is seen through the trees to the right. The trail threads its way into a narrow gorge, and the way becomes quite rocky for a short time. At 2.6 mi. (4.2 km) it becomes steep for 50 yds. (47 m) before bursting out onto open rock.

The rest of the ascent is a long, gradual to moderate grade over open rock with occasional dips into wooded gullies. White pines are dispersed on the slopes, and blueberries are everywhere. Large rock cairns guide you. Views begin to open up behind you to the east as you climb. Vermont's Green Mountains are profiled on the distant horizon, and careful observers can catch glimpses of Lake Champlain.

A rim is reached at 3.0 mi. (4.9 km), where you gain your first sighting to the south and west. Magnificent Pharaoh Lake lies below you in the shadows of Pharaoh Mountain. Treadway's summit is before you, to your right front.

Some backpackers may not wish to proceed beyond this point, since there is a fairly steep col followed by a long, moderate climb to the peak's summit. However, with a few minutes rest the pack won't seem so heavy, and there's a great view to the north from the summit. The High Peaks of Mount Marcy and her court stand out in full glory to the north.

The summit is reached at 3.2 mi. (5.2 km). Summit elevation is 2248 ft. (687 m) and ascent from the last trail junction is 848 ft. (259 m). The bulk of the mountain top is milky quartz; if you look carefully, some outstanding rose quartz can be found. A long leisurely lunch has been earned, and this summit is the perfect place to enjoy it.

When you can pull yourself away, return to the Grizzle Ocean outlet junction, which will be reached at 5.0 mi. (8.1 km). Turn right at the trail junction and follow yellow trail markers. Your course parallels the outlet stream, which you soon cross. The gradual upgrade takes you to a trail junction at 5.4 mi. (8.7 km). The trail straight ahead leads 2.5 mi. (4. 1 km) to Pharaoh Lake via Wolf Pond.

Turn left from the junction and walk along a blue-marked trail 0.1 mi. (0.2 km) to the lean-to at Grizzle Ocean. The lean-to, at 5.5 mi. (8.9 km), sits back from the shore, surrounded by well-thinned trees. Across the "ocean" is Thunderbolt Mountain, an easy bushwhack. An informal path leads around the shoreline. Approximately 0.1 mi. (0.2 km) around the northwest shore is a very nice informal campsite.

The return trip to the parking area is 1.9 mi. (3.1 km). This makes a total round-trip distance, including Treadway Mountain, of 7.4 mi. (12.0 km).

Pharaoh Mountain-Pharaoh Lake Loop

Difficulty: Moderate
Round Trip Distance: 13.3 mi. (21.3 km)
Time Necessary: 2 days
Map: ADK Eastern Region map; Putnam Pond 7.5'; Paradox Lake 15'

DAY 1. Beginners who haven't learned to pace themselves may feel this is a tough hike. But if you leave yourself plenty of time for the ascent of Pharaoh Mountain and rest when necessary, you'll find this really is not a rough trip at all. Once at the summit the rest of the trip is a breeze.

Pharaoh Lake is a large lake with several lean-tos along its shorelines. It has good fishing and is rather scenic, with rocky outcrops and tall white pines displaying considerable beauty.

If approaching from the Adirondack Northway (Interstate 87), take exit 28. Follow Rte. 74 east a short distance to Rte. 9. Turn right (south) and drive 0.5 mi. (0.8 km) to a road junction. Turn left onto Alder Meadow Road. Bear left at a fork in this road 2.2 mi. (3.2 km) from Rte. 9. Travel another 1.4 mi. (2.2 km) to the parking area at the end of this road. Turn right and follow Crane Pond Road another 1.9 mi. (3.0 km) to the DEC parking area at Crane Pond. Crane Pond Road is a narrow dirt road offering good skiing in the winter. Technically, Crane Pond Road has been closed, but due to local unrest, authorities have temporarily permitted vehicles to use it if seasonal weather permits. The hiker should be aware that 1.9 mi. (3.1 km) additional walking in each direction may be required if authorities decide to enforce earlier decisions.

Sign in at the trail register (0.0 mi.). The top of Pharaoh Mountain is 2.8 mi. (4.5 km) away. A 1257 ft. (384 m) ascent is required to reach the 2556 ft. (782 m) summit. Be sure to take plenty of water.

Cross the foot bridge over Crane Pond outlet and follow red DEC trail markers up an old logging road to the south. Soon you will be in the Pharaoh Lake Wilderness Area. The attractive mixed wood forest has easy, enjoyable ups and downs.

A trail junction is reached at 0.7 mi. (1.1 km). The Pharaoh Mountain trail makes a sharp right and then a left across a bridge before straightening out again. The lower slopes of the mountain give no trouble, but the grade progressively steepens as you climb. Take shorter steps and rest your pack occasionally. You are encouraged to follow the hiking trail rather than the steeper telephone line.

In the upper third of the mountain, you will cross a rocky creek. Though the stream may be dry in the summer, there is usually water coming from a large rock in the stream. This is the last water before the summit.

The trail now becomes very rocky. Views begin to open up to the west. Goose Pond may be visible behind you to the north. One last, steep incline brings you to the fire observer's cabin site and base of the former tower.

Spectacle Pond, Desolate Brook, and other bodies of water are to the west. You may be fortunate enough to see turkey vultures gliding above the cliffs to your left front. By going a short distance southwest to another vantage point, you get a good view of Pharaoh Lake.

This summit makes a good snowshoe trip of 9.4 mi. (15.2 km) round trip from the winter parking area. Some people ski to the base of the mountain before donning snowshoes for the ascent.

The descent to Pharaoh Lake begins at a trail to the rear of the fire observer's cabin site. It initially heads eastward before swinging to the south. The upper section is quite steep in places as the trail cuts between large boulders. These moss-covered giants are most interesting. At approximately 3.3 mi. (5.3 km), a ledge provides good viewing. The trail now levels for awhile. The rocky route follows a ridge contour that offers fine vistas to the east.

At 3.7 mi. (6.0 km) the trail again begins a moderate grade descent, which continues to the lake shore. A trail junction is reached about 50 ft. (15 m) from the lake. You'll probably want to continue to the boat landing to get a refreshing drink of water and take a well deserved rest by the shore. What appears to be the opposite side of the lake is actually a large island.

Climbing the short distance back up the trail, turn left (south). The red-marked trail continues well above the water, generally following the contours of the land. Occasional minor knolls are crossed until you again find yourself near the shoreline of the lake at 5.3 mi. (8.6 km).

Here, a trail junction is found. To the left, a yellow-marked trail leads back along the peninsula to a lean-to, which is reached at 5.6 mi. (9.0 km). It is 200 ft. (61 m) from the end of the peninsula. The setting is magnificent. To sit on the tip of this peninsula in the early morning, watching the mist rise as ducks and loons swim around the lake, is an experience not soon forgotten.

DAY 2. Retrace the 0.4 mi. (0.6 km) to the trail junction. Continue southward along the red-marked trail. The terrain becomes more rugged, but still is not difficult. At approximately 0.9 mi. (1.5 km) the attentive hiker will spot a lean-to along the shoreline, several meters through the trees. No side trail is immediately evident, so some care is needed or you will miss it. Again you veer away from the water and gain some elevation. Some bare rock outcrops are crossed before the trail drops down to the bridge over the outlet of Pharaoh Lake at 1.2 mi. (1.9 km).

Just before crossing the bridge, you'll notice a trail cutting back sharply to the right rear. It leads to a spring, which doesn't always flow clearly. Across the bridge is a grassy slope that looks like it has always been there. Actually, this little meadow is where an interior ranger's station stood for many years. It was removed in 1978 to make the region better conform to the legal definition of wilderness, wherein manmade permanent structures should not be found.

An old logging road bears to the right. Today, it is a foot trail leading approximately 3.0 mi. (4.9 km) to Beaver Pond Road near Brant Lake. This is the closest direct route to Pharaoh Lake from a road.

The trail around the lake continues to the left, heading up a gradual slope, now following a yellow-marked horse trail. After a short distance you reach a barn with stalls for horse backpacking trips. Nearby are two lean-tos, used primarily by horseback riders.

Proceeding along the logging road, a double-sized lean-to is found after a 10-minute walk.

At 2.2 mi. (3.6 km), a short distance from this lean-to, a junction is reached. The hiking trail forks to the left toward the lakeshore, whereas the horse trail continues to the right along the road to Springhill Ponds. Keep a sharp lookout for this turnoff. After crossing a small stream, a side trail leads to a lean-to near the lake. Informal campsites dot this section of the lakeshore.

The trail steepens at 2.8 mi. (4.5 km). You are soon high above the lake, sidling along a steep-sided ridge. As you descend again toward the water, you can see a large beaver house in the bay. The trail levels a bit and is easier for walking.

A trail junction appears at 3.2 mi. (5.2 km). The trail coming in from the right leads 2.5 mi. (4.1 km) to Grizzle Ocean via Wolf Pond. Bearing to the left, continue northward toward Winter Green Point. At approximately 3.6 mi. (5.8 km) the route swings around the end of the bay and heads westward until the last lean-to on the lake is reached at 3.9 mi. (6.3 km). This nice lean-to makes a good place for a lunch or rest stop.

The route from the lean-to leads northward around Split Rock Bay. This huge cleaved boulder stands like a sentinel in the narrow bay. A deliciously cool spring comes out of the slope on the right at 4.1 mi. (6.6 km). Here, at the tip of the bay, is a good place to fill up on water before beginning the steep climbing just ahead.

A few minutes after leaving the spring you start a moderately steep ascent up a grade for 0.2 mi. (0.3 km). Some conveniently placed boulders near the top of grade, 300 ft. (92 m) above the lake surface, make good seats to rest on.

The trail takes you to the northwest along the eastern base of Pharaoh Mountain. Nearly level for the first 0.5 mi. (0.8 km), it thereafter becomes a gradual downgrade and eases your travel for the remaining distance to Crane Pond. It is a very enjoyable stretch of trail, though past strong winds have caused frequent blowdown of aging beeches in several places.

A junction is reached at 6.0 mi. (9.7 km). The red-marked trail to the right leads 0.5 mi. (0.8 km) to Crab Pond and 1.2 mi. (1.9 km) to Horseshoe Pond. From Horseshoe Pond it is possible to loop over to Lilypad Pond. Beyond Lilypad Pond, one can hike northwest to Rte. 74 or connect into the Putnam Pond area via Rock Pond.

Continuing straight ahead on the yellow-marked trail, you cross the inlet to Glidden Marsh on a bridge at 6.3 mi. (10.2 km). Soon Glidden Marsh appears on the left. This is a beautiful body of water, teeming with wildlife. There are numerous beaver dams, and birdlife abounds. You view the open water through magnificent white birches as you walk along an old woods road on the northeast side of the marsh.

The trail to Oxshoe Pond enters from the right at 6.7 mi. (10.9 km). Oxshoe Pond is 0.3 mi. (0.5 km); a lean-to is found on its southern shoreline.

The trail ahead narrows as it passes along the left side of a wet area. It then swings over a small rise and soon comes to the Pharaoh Mountain junction at 7.0 mi. (11.3 km).

Bear right and walk along the grassy road 0.7 mi. (1.1 km) to Crane Pond. The parking area is reached at 7.7 mi. (12.5 km).

Pharaoh Lake

Fifth Peak ▲

Tongue Mt. Range

Mother Bunch Isles

Elephant Mt. ▲

To Pine Bk. Rd.

French Point Mt. ▲

Black Mt. ▲

Round Pond

Black Mt. Pond

Lapland Pond

First Peak ▲

Lake George

Milman Pond

The Narrows

Erebus Mt. ▲

Greenland Pond

Fishbrook Pond

Shelving Rock

Shelving Rock Mt. ▲

Sleeping Beauty Mt. ▲

Bumps Pond

Spectacle Pond

Shelving Rock Rd.

Dacy Clearing

Little Buck Mt. ▲

P

N

Buck Mt. ▲

Hogtown

Pilot Knob

P

0   ½   1

Scale in miles

To Rt. 149

To South Bay Rd. and Fort Ann

Lake George Wild Forest Area

2. The Lake George Wild Forest Area

The east side of Lake George is a little-known section of the Adirondack Park. You don't find yourself there by accident; you have to head into this isolated country by design. Filled with historical interest, its 30-plus miles of hiking trails make it a place worth heading for.

The Lake George-Lake Champlain Corridor is where much of both the French and Indian and the Revolutionary wars was bitterly fought. Only the flitting shadows of Roger's Rangers were seen on cold winter nights as the scouts headed north on forays. And it was here in the dead of winter that Henry Knox struggled down frozen Lake George, transporting Fort Ticonderoga's cannon to besiege Boston. It's not hard to imagine Mohawk warriors paddling a tortured Father Isaac Jogues to martyrdom at Ossernenon on the Mohawk River.

The woods seem full of the spirits of Duncan Campbell, Colonel Munro, and the Marquis de Montcalm. To a student of American history it is hard to imagine a more fascinating activity than reliving the past from atop one of the lake's open mountain peaks.

In the midst of this Yorker heritage are over 30 lakes and ponds surrounded by hemlocks, pines, and birch. Beaver are found on every body of water. Ducks fly in and out continually. There are mountains to climb and the fishing is good.

The Lake George Wild Forest Area straddles the central portion of Lake George. Trails in the Tongue Mountain Range on the west side of the lake are not recommended for summer backpacking because there is no water to be found on the high trails that follow down the spine of the range. Much summer day hiking is done here, however, since the small amounts of water needed for a day hike can easily be carried. (Refer to *An Adirondack Sampler: Day Hikes for All Seasons*, published by ADK.) The Tongue Range does provide excellent snowshoe backpacking in the winter, when snow can be melted for water.

The part of the Wild Forest Area that is on the east side of Lake George is quite different. Here an ideal environment and almost limitless trails provide rewarding outings.

There is an occasional report of rattlesnakes at Shelving Rock and on Black Mountain in the summer months but, while some care should be taken in these two areas, the hiker should not be unduly concerned. As a precaution, look at the far side of logs before stepping over them, and be careful where you place your hands when climbing steep rocky zones.

There are three access points to the hiking areas on the east side of Lake George: Pilot Knob, Shelving Rock Road, and Huletts Landing. All three are best reached from Interstate 87, exit 20, at Lake George. Turn left onto Rte. 9, then turn right toward Whitehall when you reach Rte. 149.

If you wish to go to Pilot Knob, proceed along Rte. 149 until you reach Rte. 9L, just past a golf course. Turn left onto Rte. 9L and travel northward until you come to a right-hand turn for Pilot Knob and Katterkill Bay. This is Pilot Knob Road. Drive approximately 3.0 mi. (4.9 km) along Pilot Knob Road to the DEC parking lot and signpost on the right side of the road.

The DEC parking area on Shelving Rock Road is best reached by driving along Rte. 149 toward Whitehall. After Rte. 9L, continue on Rte. 149 for 1.5 mi. (2.4 km) until you reach Buttermilk Falls Road. This road is on the left; there is a store called The Black Rooster at the intersection. From here it is 9.8 mi. (15.9 km) to the Shelving Rock parking area. Buttermilk Falls is seen behind a home on the left at 1.4 mi. (2.3 km), and the road merges into Sly Pond Road at 4.1 mi. (6.6 km). The DEC Inman Pond trail up Buck Mountain is passed on the left at 6.5 mi. (10.5 km). Continue to the Hogtown Road intersection at 9.0 mi. (14.6 km). Continue straight ahead on the road you have been traveling for another 0. 8 mi. (1.3 km) until you reach the DEC parking area, where a large sign reads "Lake George Horse Trails."

This parking area can also be reached from Fort Ann. In Fort Ann, turn off Rte. 4 onto County Road 16 (Charles St.) at the Portage Restaurant. This road leads towards South Bay through a most attractive rural valley. A large open gravel pit is passed 5.9 mi. (9.6 km) from Fort Ann. Hogtown Road is reached 0.3 mi. (0.5 km) past this gravel pit. Make a left-hand turn onto this road, which has no identifying sign. This is a very narrow unpaved road which can be in poor condition during the spring mud season. The Buttermilk Falls Road described above is a much better route.

The Huletts Landing DEC parking area is reached by following Rte. 149 to Fort Ann. Turn left onto Rte. 4 and drive to Whitehall. Continue through Whitehall, where the road you have been traveling on becomes Rte. 22. Approximately 4.5 mi. (7.3 km) north of the point where Rte. 22 crosses Lake Champlain's South Bay you will reach the road for Huletts Landing. Turn left and proceed 2.7 mi. (4.4 km) to Pike Brook Road. Turn left again and travel another 0.8 mi. (1.3 km) on Pike Brook Road. As you begin to descend a hill, the parking area and a large DEC sign is seen on the right. This is 3.5 mi. (5.6 km) from Rte. 22.

This region offers a wide variety of backpacking opportunities. The length of time available, pace desired, and specific activities to be carried out will all affect your final selection of route. A map has been provided to help you make your decision.

Following are detailed trail descriptions of two rather lengthy trips into this country. While not everyone will have the time or inclination to do each of these in their entirety, most of the trail system in this area has been described. From them you will be able to put together outings tailored to your own needs and interests. For additional information, see ADK's *Guide to Adirondack Trails: Eastern Region*.

No unassigned overnight camping is permitted along the Lake George shoreline from Shelving Rock to Black Mountain Point. Arrangements to camp there must be made through the DEC in the same manner that one obtains camping spots on the state-owned islands of Lake George.

Travel from the lakeshore inland is uphill and moderately steep. Black Mountain Pond, for instance, is approximately 1400 ft. (428 m) above Lake George. North-south routes are relatively less strenuous than are east–west routes. The shoreline trails are best hiked in the spring or early fall before hunting season opens. At these times you will have the trails to yourself. At other times, hunters or boat campers may detract from your enjoyment, since differing activities are not always compatible.

Fishbrook Pond and Sleeping Beauty Mountain
Difficulty: Moderate
Round Trip Distance: 12.7 mi. (20.6 km)
Time Necessary: 2 days
Map: Bolton Landing 15' Series

Fishbrook Pond and Sleeping Beauty Mountain make an ideal backpacking trip for a weekend outing. The trailhead is at the DEC parking area on Shelving Rock Road. The route is generally along an old horse road with varied terrain. This would also make a good winter cross-country ski trip, though snowmobiles may be encountered. Be sure to sign the trail register. Trailhead elevation is 1309 ft. (400 m).

Always follow the small circular foot trail markers. Horse trail markers (with a horsehead on them) and snowmobile markers (about twice as large as the others) will also be seen. Since the horse and snowmobile trails often coincide with the foot trails, a watchful eye is needed to maintain the proper route.

The trail to Fishbrook Pond follows yellow trail markers from the barrier (0.0 mi.) at the rear of the parking area. The gravel road has minor ups and downs . At 0.5 mi. (0.8 km) a small DEC signpost is passed. Another 200 ft. (61 m) along the trail is a junction where a yellow-marked horse trail bears to the left. Avoid it.

Continuing along your route, Dacy Clearing is reached at 2.2 mi. (3.6 km). Just as you enter the clearing, another dirt road comes in from the left. It has yellow horse trail markers and heads to the east.

Dacy Clearing is an interesting place. Foundations of an old homestead are seen at various points around the clearing. A few tie-up railings for horses are also scattered here and there. Standing out starkly against the distant sky, the reclining profile of Sleeping Beauty Mountain presents an inviting vista to the north. One of the finest views in the Lake George region can be had from this great precipice.

Dacy Clearing is constricted in the middle and so really is almost two clearings. Your route crosses the first one before circling down a small grade to a stream. A bridge is found here and from it the road winds upward to the second clearing. It is evident that this site is sometimes used for camping, but only an emergency should make its use necessary. At the far end of the open area, somewhat hidden by the trees on the left side, a blue markered horse trail leads 3.1 mi. (5.0 km) to Shelving Rock Road.

Another barrier blocks the north end of the clearing. You have now traveled 2.5 mi. (4.1 km); this is a good place to take a break before beginning the next section. Beyond the barrier, a rock-filled road angles up the side of the ridge in broad switchbacks toward Sleeping Beauty Mountain. Before the next junction is reached, 500 ft. (152 m) elevation will be gained.

The junction is reached at 3.4 mi. (5.5 km). The yellow-marked trail turns abruptly to the right onto what appears to be a broad rolling trail. After about 0.2 mi. (0.3 km), however, this old bridal path begins a series of steep switchbacks that make for a rather rugged ascent if you are toting a full backpack. It is therefore recommended that you use instead the red-marked trail straight past this junction and continue on to Bumps Pond. Sleeping Beauty Mountain should be climbed, but it will be surmounted far more easily if climbed from the north by its other trail on the return trip.

Steady climbing commences immediately on the red-marked trail, but at a moderate grade. Two excellent lookouts to the southwest are passed. Height of land is reached at 2160 ft. (661 m). You have gained 952 ft. (291 m) since leaving the parking area.

The trail drops in elevation and circles the west side of Bumps Pond, where a chimney is all that remains of a cabin. A junction (somewhat flooded due to beaver activity) is a short distance past the chimney, at 4.4 mi. (7.1 km).

A DEC sign states (erroneously) that it is 0.6 mi. (1.0 km) to Erebus Mountain. Actually, a yellow-marked trail leads 0.3 mi. (0.5 km) to a fine view of Lake George at Bumps Pond Lookout, and from there an unofficially marked, semi-bushwhack heads off for approximately another 1.5 mi. (2.4 km) to the summit of Erebus Mountain. If you decide to take this side trip to Bumps Pond Lookout, be sure to take the fork that angles up the slope to the right. Avoid the horse trail which stays on the level.

The main trail continues northward. A shortcut through the neck of a road curve makes a nice place to rest. A large log marks the location of what was once a very nice spring. It needs to be cleaned out and is not recommended for drinking from at this time.

The red-marked trail ends at 4.2 mi. (6.8 km), where it again meets the yellow-marked trail that comes down off Sleeping Beauty Mountain. This is the trail up the mountain that you should take on the return trip.

Bumps Pond Outlet is followed for a brief span. Considerable beaver activity is noted. Following yellow markers, a gradual descent occurs until you pass through a small hollow. Then the slope becomes moderate and remains so until Fishbrook Pond is reached.

Almost before you realize you are there, both Fishbrook Pond and its first lean-to appear at 5.2 mi. (8.4 km). The setting is most attractive. Firewood is scarce, however, and you are advised to pack in a camp stove if you plan to camp there.

Directly across the pond, a second lean-to stands alone on a picturesque open point. The trail to it leads around the east shoreline of the pond. The pond's outlet is crossed by a bridge not far from the first lean-to. At the northern end of the pond a major trail junction is located at 5.6 mi. (9.1 km). Turning left (west), the second lean-to is 0.1 mi. (0.2 km) along the red-marked trail.

Trails north of the junction are described below in the Black Mountain and South Loop section. The red trail west heads down to Black Mountain Point on Lake George.

DAY 2. For the return trip, backtrack 1.4 mi. (2.3 km) to the yellow-marked trail up Sleeping Beauty Mountain, which drops off the shoulder of the road at Bumps Pond Outlet (0.0 mi.). The climb from this route is very easy and should not be missed.

Crossing the outlet on top of a beaver dam, you can see several dams in the direction of the pond. The trail then climbs gradually towards the summit. Several switchbacks are negotiated and the trail becomes a moderate grade. When the leaves are off the trees, fairly good views to the east are available near the summit. The trail passes just beneath the wooded peak at approximately 0.5 mi. (0.8 km). From here it descends slightly and continues along the ridge with comfortable ups and downs.

After another 10 minutes of walking, a trail joins at an acute angle from the left. There is no sign, but small arrows have been carved into the trees. Continue straight ahead. The trail climbs gradually for another 100 yds. (92 m), where it terminates at an open lookout with a marvelous view. The lookout is at the 1.1 mi. (1.8 km) point.

To the southeast is a wide straight valley, leading straight to Fort Ann. Glacial Lake Vermont once connected Lake Champlain with points south, and this unusual Adirondack valley remains as a remnant of the past. Just to its right is Mount Hope. The highest mountain to the south of you is Buck Mountain. Further right to the southwest is Little Buck Mountain. Lake George stretches out before you to the east, with Bolton Landing on the distant shore. Shelving Rock Mountain, like an inverted soup bowl, is due east of you. Northwest Bay goes behind the Tongue Mountain Range across the lake. Crane Mountain with its flat top stands out in the distant southwest. The Adirondack high peaks are seen over the Tongue Mountain Range to the northwest. If you move around to the extreme left of the lookout you can see northeastward into the mountains of Vermont.

To descend the mountain, return 0.1 mi. (0.2 km) to the trail junction you passed just before reaching the lookout. The trail to the right drops down a moderate grade through a series of switchbacks. You curve around, finally arriving directly below the steep cliffs of the lookout. These rocks are most impressive. The stonework seen at various points was originally built to make the trail passable for horses, though this route is not suitable for equestrians today. The junction is reached after walking 1.2 mi. (1.9 km), making the whole Sleeping Beauty trail a total of 2.3 mi. (3.7 km). From this junction you return along the same route you came in on for another 3.4 mi. (5.5 km) to the Shelving Rock Road parking area.

Black Mountain and South Loop

Difficulty: Moderate to difficult
Round Trip Distance: 14.2 mi. (23.0 km)
Time Necessary: 2 days
Map: Bolton Landing 15' Series

The trailhead (0.0 mi.) is at the rear of the Huletts Landing DEC parking area on Pike Brook Road. Climbing a short distance, you almost immediately reach a dirt road. Turn left (west) and follow it and red trail markers 0.9 mi. (1.5 km) to a junction with a DEC signpost. The fire tower on Black Mountain can be seen from this point.

Leaving the dirt road, your trail forks to the right and skirts some private property. Stay to the trail here. The smaller woods road has a gradual grade and passes through attractive hardwoods. Continue to follow red foot trail markers. Ignore the larger snowmobile markers, which you will also see.

Another junction is reached at 1.3 mi. (2.1 km). A sign on a tree indicates the direction to Lapland Pond. Turn left (south) here and begin an easy descent which ends at a bridge over a pretty brook.

Crossing the brook, you regain some of the lost elevation as you follow a stream up a valley. A small sign on a tree at the 2.2 mi. (3.6 km) point indicates you have reached the junction, where a side trail leads 0.2 mi. (0.3 km) to the lean-to at Lapland Pond. This side trail bears left, crosses a small stream, and winds around the east side of the pond. There may be some difficulty following the trail in places, but if you keep to the edge of the pond you'll soon arrive at the lean-to.

Lapland Pond is very appealing, though heavily used. Sitting high above the pond, a sloping rock massif slants down to the water's edge. As on most ponds in this region, a beaver house is seen and birdlife abounds. The heavily occupied lean-to has little firewood available. You are reminded that only dead and down wood may be chopped up for firewood. A camp stove is advisable.

From the Lapland Pond lean-to side trail junction it is only 0.2 mi. (0. 3 km) to a major trail crossing. At 2.4 mi. (3.9 km) this trail intersection has a yellow-marked route that bears right in the direction of Round Pond. Yellow markers also bear left and head south to Milman Pond. Some care has to be taken here, since the trail junction is swampy and the signs seem to be scattered about in a somewhat random fashion.

The path to Milman Pond hugs the west side of Lapland Pond. This section of trail is truly a woods path, and one must keep track of the trail markers. A stream is crossed where beaver runs make it seem the trail bears right. However, the correct way swings left around the flooded section.

At about 3.0 mi. (4.9 km) a snowmobile trail is reached at a T-intersection. Turn right (west) and follow it up a moderate grade to a small stream crossing. Take care not to continue up the grade along the snowmobile route, once across the stream. Instead, the hiking trail abruptly turns left and follows the stream uphill.

Leveling off at the top of the rise, you see Milman Pond below you to the right. Before long, you drop down toward the water and at 4.3 mi. (7.0 km) reach the Milman Pond lean-to. This is a newer type lean-to, precut and air-dropped into the site. It's interesting to compare lean-to styles; although they all appear alike at first glance, you'll see the personal mark of the builder in the details of each structure. An experienced hiker can often tell you, simply from these details, who built a particular lean-to.

The terrain changes after leaving Milman Pond. Passing over a ridge line, the woods open somewhat. You follow a land contour for awhile; then you climb over the divide and gradually lose elevation as you approach Fishbrook Pond. The more open forest is a nice variation in scenery.

Greenland Pond junction is reached at 5.3 mi. (8.6 km). This side trail follows red trail markers northeastward for 1.0 mi. (1.6 km) to the north end of Greenland Pond. From there a less maintained path strikes northward to intersect the snowmobile trail, east of where the Lapland Pond trail cuts into it.

The yellow-marked trail you have been following continues 0.3 mi. (0.5 km) southward to another junction. It appears that the trail would go straight ahead, but it doesn't. Instead it drops diagonally down a slope to the right to the shore of Fishbrook Pond, where there is a major junction at the 5.6 mi. (9.1 km) point.

A red-marked foot trail leads 0.2 mi. (0.3 km) around the north shore to a lean-to which sits out on an open point. The yellow-marked foot trail proceeds southward along the east shoreline. At 5.9 mi. (9.6 km) Fishbrook Pond Outlet is crossed on a bridge. Still following the shoreline, you reach a second lean-to at 6.0 mi. (9.7 km). Fishbrook Pond makes an ideal camping area from which several possible trips can originate.

The route suggested here returns 3.6 mi. (5.8 km) to the junction described at the 2.4 mi. (3 .9 km) mark. Using this junction as a starting point (0.0 mi.), one can return to the Pike Brook Road parking area by circling the base and then going over Black Mountain.

The yellow trail turns westward from this junction, passing over a small divide to Round Pond, which appears after 0.3 mi. (0.5 km) of walking. Another small rise is broached before you drop down to Black Mountain Pond at 0.7 mi. (1.1 km). On its north shore, several meters upslope from the shore, a nice lean-to keeps watch over this little jewel of water.

Continuing eastward another 0.3 mi. (0.5 km), the trail junction from

Black Mountain Point on Lake George joins your route. To the left, a red trail descends 1400 ft. (428 m) in 2.0 mi. (3.2 km) to the lake shore.

The way to the summit of Black Mountain swings uphill to the right, past this intersection, and follows red trail markers. You encounter several switchbacks as the moderate grade steepens. You will gain 936 ft. (286 m) in elevation before reaching the fire tower at its peak. Views of Lake George soon begin to appear. The summit is reached at 1.8 mi. (2.9 km), and there are vistas in all directions. Tongue Mountain Range is directly across the lake, with the Adirondack high peaks beyond. Lake Champlain's South Bay and Vermont are to the northeast. Almost the entire length of Lake George's 32 mi. (51.8 km) are visible from this summit. Summit elevation is 2646 ft. (809 m).

It is 2.8 mi. (4.5 km) from the top of Black Mountain back to the Pike Brook Road parking area. The trail descends past the fire observer's cabin and then enters the woods to the east. A short, steep rock face is negotiated before the trail moderates to a more relaxing rate of descent. A pleasant woods road, which passes a rushing stream and then a quiet spring, is soon reached on the left.

At 3.3 mi. (5.3 km) the Lapland Pond junction is reached. It comes in from the right. From here it is 1.3 mi. (2.1 km) back to the parking area. At 4.6 mi. (7.5 km), a right-hand turn takes you down the brief slope to the parking area.

Looking north from Black Mountain Point

3. The Siamese Ponds Wilderness Area

Much of the Forest Preserve approximates true wilderness more today than it did a century ago: the trails by which we now enter and enjoy this returning wilderness were created by man's original encroachment. Early lumbermen bought huge land tracts for only a few cents an acre, lumbered the forest, and then abandoned the land, refusing to pay taxes. The state eventually reclaimed these sites. Homesteaders who had purchased cleared land from lumbermen found the short growing season and thin topsoil of the North Country difficult; frequently they, too, gave up their inholdings and left.

Time has replaced the forests so abused by the early lumber kings. Natural tree successions are gradually returning the woods to its original state. The scars of the past are slowly being obliterated.

The Siamese Ponds Wilderness Area is part of this Forest Preserve. The Siamese Ponds trail follows much of the old stage coach road Bill Wakely talked the state into building from North Creek to Baker's Mills. The trail heading west from Old Farm Clearing was the main route to Indian Lake in the 1840s. Only the unexpected presence of apple blossoms in the spring of the year remain to remind us that Burnt Shanty Clearing was once a homestead. Curtis Clearing, Hayden Mountain, Hayes Flow, and Big Hopkins Mountain give clues as to whom we might have met a century ago in this country. Botheration Pond, Balm of Gilead Mountain, Ruby Mountain, Chatiemac Lake, and the Kunjamuk all suggest things about the kinds of people they were. For a brief time man intruded and then stole away, leaving only names to entice the curious to ponder bygone days.

Buildings burn down, corduroy rots, hayfields become deer meadows, and memories fade as the shadows of time lengthen and blur man's perceptions of the past. Only the old roads remain to provide us entry into this land and back to another era. Without them, few people would venture here to witness the return of wilderness. Perhaps man's temporary intrusion had a purpose, quite unknown to the inhabitants in their time.

The Siamese Ponds Wilderness Area has numerous trails and endless bush-whacking possibilities. Sprinkled among the over 100,000 acres of rolling hills are a few mountains of the 3000 ft. (917 m) class and many smaller summits and bumps. Sixty-seven bodies of water are found here.

See the Adirondack Mountain Club's *Guide to Adirondack Trails: Central Region* for a comprehensive description of the Siamese Ponds Wilderness Area. The ADK map "Trails of the Central Region" might also be useful.

The Siamese Ponds Trail

Difficulty: Easy, with a few long, challenging grades
Round Trip Distance: 12.6 mi. (20.4 km)
Time Necessary: 2 days
Map: Thirteenth Lake 15' Series, Thirteenth Lake metric

The Siamese Ponds Trail provides a variety of terrain and beauty that should satisfy any backpacker. The beginner will find a generally easy route with enough hardships at times to make him aware that "easy" is a relative term. The experienced trekker will recognize the infinite possibilities for side trips, fishing, and nature study. The more hearty types can step off the trail at almost any point to be swallowed up in true wilderness isolation where only the experienced should venture. Cross-country skiers and snowshoers find this a winter wonderland. Skiers usually make the run south from Thirteenth Lake to Rte. 8. It's a good day's through trip, with the last long down grade for the expert class only. The rest of the trip is relatively easy, though long. Spring snow lasts a long time here.

The trailhead is on the west side of Rte. 8, 4.0 mi. (6.5 km) south of Baker's Mills. A large wooden DEC signpost marks the spacious parking area. (Be sure to examine the older metal Forest Preserve signpost located at the opposite side of the parking area.) Trailhead elevation is 1760 ft. (538 m). Blue foot trail markers and yellow ski markers lead you up a trail at the rear of the parking area. The well-constructed shelter protecting the trail register is the first of many indicators that this is a very well-maintained trail.

Gradual grades soon steepen as you circle up to the saddle crossing the ridge that constitutes Eleventh Mountain. Beginning so early in the hike, this 15-minute ascent clearly informs you of your physical condition. The 0.3 mi. (0.5 km) distance gains 240 ft. (73 m) elevation.

Near the top of the grade, you may notice an old road merging with your trail from the left. This is a remnant of the old stage coach road from Baker's Mills to North Creek. The welcome easy grades you'll follow to the Sacandaga lean-to pretty much stay to this highway of the past.

A long gradual descent ensues through hardwoods. At 1.5 mi. (2.4 km) you reach the Diamond Brook bridge, where Diamond Brook flows off Diamond Mountain through a wide, flat area. This is usually a rough place to get past in the spring, when meltwaters overflow the stream channel. Bear left and you'll soon pick up the trail again. You also reach the East Branch of the Sacandaga River. This most pleasant stream will occupy your attention as you follow along its left bank, walking upstream. Soon you reach a beaver meadow where you can look northward to the diamond-shaped mountain from whence Diamond Brook gets its name.

The almost grown-in Burnt Shanty Clearing is reached at 2.7 mi. (4.4 km). The trail continues to parallel the East Branch of the Sacandaga, though sight of it is not quite as frequent now. The almost level route gives you much opportunity to enjoy your surroundings.

Siamese Ponds Wilderness Area

There is a trail junction at 3.5 mi. (5 .7 km). The right fork leads another 5.5 mi. (8.9 km) to Old Farm Clearing and Thirteenth Lake.

Take the left fork. It leads 0.5 mi. (0.8 km) to the Sacandaga lean-to, where a bridge crosses over the East Branch of the Sacandaga. This is a most attractive place. The lean-to sits on a flat area a few feet above the river surface, giving you a commanding view of the waterway and points northward. The breezes emanating from the river provide a welcome sensation as you sit on the lean-to's deacon seat, drinking in the rewarding sights along with some of the cool river water.

The bridge is somewhat of an enigma. It is a beautiful suspension bridge, airlifted to its present location in 1967. It is clearly needed here. However, concrete and steel in a wilderness area make the believer of true wilderness ethics blush with chagrin. The best that one can do is to say it is the exception that proves the rule.

The neophyte hiker who is all tuckered out will probably decide this is about as idyllic a spot to stay as can be found, and will leave Siamese Ponds for a packless side trip before heading back out the next morning.

Siamese Ponds lies 2.3 mi. (3.7 km) to the west, across the bridge. As you hike along, you are at first so occupied with the glimpses of beaver activity seen through the trees at your right that you don't notice you're gaining elevation. The rolling terrain slowly rises as you skirt the lower shoulder of Siamese Mountain. Siamese Brook is the large stream that you cross after about 15 minutes walking. It's a good place for a refreshing drink. Before height of land is reached at about the 6.0 mi. (10.0 km) point, over 425 ft. (130 m) elevation is gained.

Siamese Ponds is soon seen below you to the right. A good campsite is passed just before you reach the shoreline, where a second, smaller site is found at the shoreline of the lower pond. This is a very pretty sheet of water. At times, a strong breeze is felt as the fetch wind whips down the pond's distance. It's the sort of place where you want to sit awhile and perhaps watch the birds flit over the water as the clouds drift by overhead. You might be tempted to throw out a fishing line as an excuse to remain there reading a book for the rest of the day.

It would be best to camp at one of the previously mentioned locations. However, a hike to the upper pond is encouraged because it will strikingly illustrate what beavers can do to an ecosystem. Crossing the pond's outlet, walk along the very edge of the west shoreline, following a narrow path. As beavers have methodically dammed up the outlet of the lower pond, the pond has progressively enlarged.

You'll enjoy the long descent on the way back to the Sacandaga lean-to. Allow plenty of time, however, for regaining the 400 ft. (122 m) elevation that you lost between Diamond Brook and the col on Eleventh Mountain. Look for the cliffs as you begin this climb. Then keep an eye out for where the old stage coach road branches off to the right as you drop down the far side of the col toward the parking area.

Puffer Pond

Difficulty: Easy, with minor grades
Round Trip Distance: 11.0 mi. (17.8 km)
Time Necessary: 2 days
Map: Thirteenth Lake 15' Series, Thirteenth Lake metric

Puffer Pond is ideal for a backpacker's beginning hike. The grades are short, the trail is excellent, and the country cannot be surpassed. More experienced hikers may do this outing as a day hike or extend it with a side trip into Hour Pond. With a waiting vehicle at the other end of the line, Puffer Pond can be the first night's destination on a through trip to Kings Flow or John Pond.

Fine ski touring and snowshoeing is found on trails originating at this trailhead. The Puffer Pond trail requires a few stream crossings that should be easy in late winter. A through trip of about 11.0 mi. (17.8 km) to the Rte. 8 Siamese Wilderness trailhead near Baker's Mills is also frequently done, but it requires expert skill in one last section just before arriving at Rte. 8.

Trailhead access is off Rte. 28 at North River. A sign points the way to Siamese Ponds Wilderness Area. A blacktop road takes you 4.2 mi. (6.8 km) to a road fork. (Do not turn at the earlier fork for Thirteenth Lake.) A small sign indicates you should bear right here. There is a winter parking area 0.5 mi. (0.8 km) along this road and a summer parking area a quarter mile beyond that. From the summer parking area it is 1.2 mi. (1.9 km) along a woods road to Old Farm Clearing. This large clearing has a register at the far end.

Immediately to the left is the trail heading to Botheration Pond. Just beyond is a spring at the left of the trail. Walking through the tree plantation, a DEC signpost is reached at 1.3 mi. (2.1 km). Take the right fork and continue through the plantation, following blue DEC trail markers.

A few minutes later you come to a climax forest and begin a gradual descent. A major inlet of Thirteenth Lake is crossed at 2.2 mi. (3.6 km). From this low point of 1700 ft. (520 m) elevation, you will gain approximately 484 ft. (148 m) before reaching Puffer Pond.

A moderate grade develops and you head upslope. You won't travel far before the sounds of cascading water are heard. Soon, you see the outlet of Hour Brook below you to the right. Entertained by its bubbling waters, you quickly reach a col, the trail levels, and you cross Hour Pond Brook.

Turning left, you continue on the level beside the brook until a little rise brings you to a side trail on the right at 2.6 mi. (4.2 km). This side trail leads 2.0 mi. (3.2 km) to Hour Pond.

Still following the brook, you almost immediately reach a second crossing place. Hour Pond Brook makes a horseshoe turn, cutting through large rocks and forming a pretty little water slide. This is a good place to take a break and enjoy your surroundings.

Once across the brook, you encounter rolling terrain, with each new roll a bit higher than the last one. The magnificent beech, maple, and hemlock forest in this region has a number of immense trees that come close to three feet in diameter. Descending one of the humps at 3.1 mi. (5.0 km), you cross a small wet section on corduroy. (You may have to leave the trail here and circle to the right.) At 3.4 mi. (5.5 km) a beaver meadow is seen. Here, an abandoned beaver dam has broken down. The once impressive pond behind the dam has become a lovely meadow where deer doubtless abound in the dusk of evening.

Another log bridge takes you across this tributary of Hour Pond Brook. You plunge back into the woods. Summer flowers, lush ferns, hammering woodpeckers, and an occasional chattering chipmunk keep your interest as you proceed through this enjoyable forest. Then, rather suddenly, you arrive at Puffer Pond and the little side trail that leads to the first lean-to at 5.2 mi. (8.4 km).

Located at the northeast end of Puffer Pond, the lean-to looks out across the pond to the steep slopes of Puffer Mountain. A path from the lean-to soon rejoins the main trail, which follows the north shoreline. Along the way two nice campsites are passed. A murky spring is seen just before the second lean-to is reached at 5.5 mi. (8.9 km). This lean-to sits well above the water's edge near the midpoint of the pond. From it, the trail swings northward to Kings Flow and John Pond.

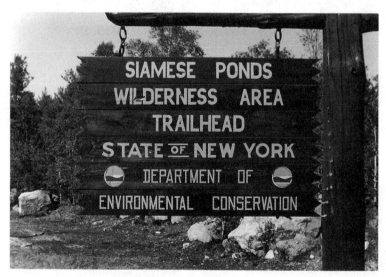

4. The Wilcox Lake Wild Forest Area

The Wilcox Lake Wild Forest Area is little known and much neglected by hikers. Hunters, anglers, and snowmobilers frequent the area, but it is deserted for much of the summer. A network of roads traverses the region, once far more populated than it is today. Some still are open to vehicles, but many now exist only as foot trails. The Oregon Trail connected the little hamlet of Oregon with Bakers Mills and points south.

Countless ponds and mountains dot the region, whetting one's curiosity with their strange names. Cod Pond, Lixard Pond, Bearpen Peak, Winona Lake, and Seneca Mountain are but a few of them.

Wilcox Lake

Difficulty: Easy
Round Trip Distance: 10.0 mi. (16.2 km)
Time: 2 days
Map: Harrisburg 15' Series, Harrisburg metric

This is an interesting trip along old logging trails through a maturing mixed wood forest. Much of the route follows the left bank of East Stony Creek. It is the kind of outing that shouldn't be hurried. Flowers abound along the streams, deer are frequently seen, and Canada geese stop over at Wilcox Lake during their migrations. Take your time and enjoy the surroundings.

Access to the trailhead is off Rte. 30 on the southern edge of the hamlet of Hope. If approaching from the direction of the Great Sacandaga Lake, turn east onto Creek Road 3.2 mi. (5.2 km) north of the DEC signpost for the Benson Section of the Northville–Placid Trail. There is a family cemetery plot at the Creek Road intersection. Drive along Creek Road 2.8 mi. (4.5 km) until you reach a road fork, where DEC signs are located. Turn left onto Mud Creek Road (Mason Road). It will become a dirt road after a few miles. A DEC signpost at the trailhead on East Stony Creek is seen on the left after driving 4.9 mi. (7.9 km). Park off the road, but avoid proceeding onto the Brownell Camp property (now the DeMunn Camp), which is privately owned and posted. Brownell's Camp has a long history as one of the early hunters' hotels in the woods. Follow the trailhead at left, along the creek, only.

From the signpost (0.0 mi.) the trail passes through private property following blue trail markers. The route you are following is a snowmobile trail in the winter, so the bridges are well constructed. Tenant Creek is crossed on one such very large bridge. (At right, the Tenant Creek Falls Trail is found just before the bridge. A fishermen's trail is seen at right, just past the bridge.)

Thereafter, you move away from streams but return to the banks of East Stony Creek at 1.1 mi. (1.8 km).

Turning right, you follow an old logging road along the left bank of East Stony Creek for almost 3.0 mi. (4.9 km). The stream is broad and moves with considerable force in the springtime. Great blocks of ice are pushed up on the shores. In summer, however, it presents a tranquil scene, with long-stemmed flowers poking through the green ferns that cloak the banks.

The grade increases at about 2.2 mi. (3.6 km), but the walking is so comfortable you don't really mind. You move away from the stream and begin to notice more conifers as elevation is gained. At just about height of land you pass out of Hamilton County and into Warren County. Gradual grades take you back downward to Dayton Creek, which is crossed at 3.1 mi. (5.0 km). If the bridge is still washed out, the creek can easily be crossed in all but the highest flows. There is a fork in the trail just beyond Dayton Creek. Take the left side of the fork, which returns you to the bank of East Stony Creek.

At 3.8 mi. (6.2 km) you come to a wide metal suspension bridge that spans East Stony Creek. This is a good lunch spot, with ducks often seen dashing along the surface of the water. Cross the bridge and carefully follow yellow snowmobile trail markers.

The trail narrows and you climb a moderate grade over the northern shoulder of Wilcox Mountain. Many fallen trees give evidence of violent storms in the past. Finally, height of land is reached at a trail junction at 4.3 mi. (7.0 km), having gained 250 ft. (76 m) elevation. Here the left-hand branch of the junction heads southwestward 4.5 mi. (7.3 km) to Willis Lake.

Turn right and head north. A jeep trail enters from the right, 0.1 mi. (0.2 km) farther along the trail. An informal campsite is found at this point. Continuing straight ahead, you find a barrier marking the end-point for vehicular travel, but irresponsible individuals sometimes drive on to the lake, anyway. Deep ruts are dug into the steep slope. Fortunately, this last section is very short. A moderately steep grade drops down to the shore of Wilcox Lake, which is reached at 4.8 mi. (7.8 km).

A DEC trail register is at the shoreline. The lake's expanse is before you, with surrounding hills casting a green sheen over the water. Two lean-tos are located on this lake. The first is 0.1 mi. (0.2 km) around the south side of the lake. It sits up above the water, the surface elevation of which is 1445 ft. (442 m). The second lean-to is to the left of the trail register, 0.2 mi. (0.3 km) around the west shoreline. It is on a small point and has several informal campsites at varying distances behind the lean-to. This second shelter is perhaps the nicer of the two shelters.

Bennett, Middle, and Murphy Lakes

Difficulty: Easy, with some moderate grades
Round Trip Distance: 6.2 mi. (10.0 km)
Time Necessary: 2 days
Map: Harrisburg 15' Series, Hope Falls metric

The route followed on this outing has existed since the early 1800s. They were still paying bounties on wolves in 1826 in the town of Hope, but boom days were ahead. Lumbering, tanning, sheep raising, and farming generated a number of thriving communities from the 1840s through the Civil War period. Then things began to slow down and the forest started to close in again. Today, the old route to Murphy Lake and Pumpkin Hollow is a snowmobile trail where old building foundations and stone walls give silent testimony to another era.

There is an attractive lean-to at Murphy Lake from which bushwhacks up surrounding peaks can easily be made. The trip is relatively short, leaving ample time for enjoying the lakes along your trail. It is a pleasant trip, which gains 540 ft. (165 m) in elevation before arriving at Murphy Lake.

Access to the trailhead is from Rte. 30 on the southern edge of the hamlet of Hope. If approaching from the direction of the Great Sacandaga Lake, turn east onto Creek Road 3.2 mi. (5.2 km) north of the DEC signpost for the Benson Section of the Northville–Placid Trail. There is a family cemetery plot at the Creek Road intersection. Drive along Creek Road 2.6 mi. (4.2 km) to the trailhead. As you descend a grade, the DEC trail sign is on the left side of the road.

Yellow foot trail markers and red snowmobile markers guide your way. The grade upward is steady. The route is rocky. After about 15 minutes, it levels somewhat but still has a gradual slope. There is evidence of lumbering in the recent past.

The trail stays above the west side of Bennett Lake, but you catch glimpses of it through the trees as you approach it. At 1.2 mi. (1.9 km) an unmarked trail forks to the right. It drops downward 0.1 mi. (0.2 km) to the sandy shore of Bennett Lake. An informal campsite is found here; this would be a good spot for a last swim on the return trip.

From the junction, the route soon begins to climb over a ridge. The increased steepness has caused vehicles traveling this route to dig up the trail quite a bit. In spite of this, the character of the forest becomes more wild. Height of land is reached at 1.7 mi. (2.8 km), and the way levels for a stretch before climbing again. At 2.2 mi. (3.6 km) the route resumes level going and stays pretty much on the contour as you walk beside a brook. The trail swings above the west side of Middle Lake. At approximately 2.6 mi. (4.2 km) an unmarked side trail leads a short distance to the shore of Middle Lake.

There is an informal campsite of sorts located here. Pickerel weed, with long purple spikes, and various lilies line the bank of this dark body of water. An island presents itself, and the distant shore has cliffs behind it. Middle Lake is quite charming.

The trail to Murphy Lake is almost level, actually descending 20 ft. (6 m) along the way. The southern end of the lake is a short 15 minutes beyond Middle Lake. After a brief walk along the east side of Murphy Lake, you reach the lean-to at 3.1 mi. (5.0 km).

The lean-to sits in a handsome grouping of hemlocks near the water. Small mountains surround the lake. Lily pads decorate its surface. The trail continues around the north end of the lake past the lean-to.

It is another 3.0 mi. (4.9 km) to Pumpkin Hollow, where a 1.7 mi. (2.8 km) drive from that trailhead will take you back to Rte. 30. If two cars are available, you may prefer a through trip. The trailhead in Pumpkin Hollow is found at the right side of a curve in the road on a small grade. A maroon-colored house (1980) is opposite the trailhead. A pull-off for parking is just a bit farther around the curve .

A small valley runs nearly north from the north end of the lake. Bush-whacks can be made up either of the small mountains at that end of the lake by following the valley about 0.2 mi. (0.3 km) to a height of land some 30 ft. (9 m) above the lake level. Once past the cliff in this valley, you can ascend either to the east or the west. The eastern climb is slightly higher. Views of Moose Mountain to the northwest and Cathead Mountain to the west are the rewards for your efforts. Be careful picking your ascent and descent routes through the rocks.

Woods road to Murphy Lake

5. The West Canada Lakes Wilderness Area

The West Canada Lakes Wilderness Area is the headwater source for three major rivers: the Cedar River flows into the Hudson; the Indian River supplies the Black River; and West Canada Creek empties into the Mohawk River.

A casual look at a map will indicate that, for the most part, this area is buffered by other state lands around it. The Moose River Recreation Area, Jessup River Wild Forest, West Canada Mountain Primitive Area, and the Pillsbury Lake Primitive Area are the primary bodies. The effect of this is that it is very difficult to get into the heart of this area and back out again in a two-day weekend trip. Hence, the West Canada Lakes and the Cedar Lakes have remained truly wild.

It is a far cry from the old days when the Belden brothers ran their secret mine on Belden Mountain, or when Lucretia Howell lived with her parents in the caves north of Spruce Lake. Bush pilot operations have terminated, and French Louie probably had as many marksmen at his West Lake camp in a single season as now frequent the place in a five-year span.

Geographical isolation hasn't been enough to prevent man from influencing the life of this region, however. Today the scourge is not the slashing lumbermen or the deer-jacking hunter. It is acid rain. In general, the higher the elevation of the land, the greater will be the amount of acidified snow and rain that will fall. Much of this region is over 2500 ft. (765 m) in elevation. Significantly, this land is also downwind of the Great Lakes, a major source of the moisture from which snow and rain form. These two factors, the Great Lakes Effect and elevation, are taking their toll. In the 1880s Traume Haskell could catch 30 or more pounds of trout through the ice of Brooktrout Lake in a single afternoon. Today it is barren of fish. Sly Pond, Wolf Lake, and other bodies of water have suffered the same fate. So far, the West Canadas and the Cedar Lakes are holding their own.

The great visual beauty of this land together with this invisible blight are difficult to focus sharply in one's mind at the same time. Nevertheless, they exist together and comprise perhaps the most upsetting worldwide problem of the present decade. Can man control himself?

The Northville-Placid Trail weaves its way through this area. The Spruce Lake trip described in this section is along part of that trail. The Brooktrout Lake trip heads into the West Canadas from the Moose River Recreation Area near Limekiln Lake. Both are excellent introductory trips to this region and can form the basis from which more extended outings may be planned. See *Guide to Adirondack Trails: West-Central Region* (ADK) for further information.

Brooktrout Lake

Difficulty: Easy, with long grades
Round Trip Distance: 10.4 mi. (16.8 km)
Time Necessary: 2 days
Map: West Canada Lake 15' Series, West Canada Lakes metric

Brooktrout Lake is a beautiful body of water nestled in the midst of sur-rounding mountains. Since trout are no longer found here, the only visitors now are a few hunters in autumn and surprisingly few backpackers. It makes a nice weekend trip or a first-night stop on a longer trek to the West Canadas.

The first half of the hike takes you up over a major ridge along an old logging road. A gentle descent makes the second half of the trip more inter-esting, and one sees evidence of beaver, deer, and bear.

Access to the trailhead is from the Limekiln Lake entrance of the Moose River Recreation Area. North of Inlet, turn off Rte. 28 at the large DEC sign for Limekiln Lake Public Campsite and Day Use Area. Continue past the campsite when you reach it on this road. The Moose River Recreation Area gateway is a short distance farther along this road. Maps are available from the ranger at the gate.

From the gate, drive 8.4 mi. (13.6 km) along the good gravel Moose River Road to a major intersection, where the road turns left for Wakely Dam. Continue straight ahead another 3.3 mi. (5.3 km) on the Otter Brook Road to a fork. Bear right and drive another 1.0 mi. (1.6 km) on the Indian Lake Road. A trailhead parking area is located on the left side of the road at a gravel pit. Signs clearly mark the spot and all intersections.

From the cable barrier at the right rear of the parking area (0.0 mi.), the trail follows a nearly level course along a grassy old logging road. Yellow trail markers will eventually guide your way, but none will be seen for quite awhile. The first of several informal camping spots appears after a few min-utes of walking as you approach the Falls Pond outlet stream.

A gradual grade that will continue at various degrees of steepness for the next 0.8 mi. (1.3 km) now begins. Along the way you will see a tremendous assemblage of hardwoods. From tamarack and small-toothed aspen to ca-noe birch and striped maple, a secondary-growth succession along the edge of the road competes with a more mature forest a few feet further into the forest.

At 1.5 mi. (2.4 km) the Falls Pond junction is reached. You may miss this junction if you're not looking for it. Falls Pond, with its informal campsite, is 0.4 mi. (0.6 km) up the side trail to the right.

As you continue straight ahead, the grade often changes but is always upward. From one open high spot the trail sweeps around a curve, giving you a fine view of the wetland grasses and spiring black spruces along Wolf Creek in the distance below you. You then drop down a bit and pass an attractive beaver pond.

Ascending again, you cross the bridge over Wolf Creek as the rushing

To Limekiln Lake

To Wakely Dam

To Indian Lake

P

N

Falls Pond

Wolf Lake

Twin Lakes

Deep Lake

Brooktrout Lake

To Cedar Lakes

West Lake

Former Ranger Station Site

0   ½   1
Scale in miles

To South Lake

West Canada Lakes Wilderness Area

water shoots through a narrow flume under you. An informal campsite is located here. Some 140 yds. (128 m) farther along the trail, you come to the Wolf Lake and Deep Lake trail junction at 2.2 mi. (3.6 km). A single side trail to these lakes heads off to the left. It forks a short distance later. Each lake is 1.0 mi. (1.6 km) from the junction. (Neither of these trails is currently maintained, and travel on them must be considered a bushwhack of sorts. Unless you are skilled in land navigation by compass and wish to experience a wet, rough outing, use of these two trails is not encouraged.)

The trail again gradually ascends over a base of glacial scoured bedrock. Finally, on a broad curve, height of land is reached. Elevation at this point is approximately 2650 ft. (810 m). You have ascended nearly 600 ft. (183 m) since leaving the parking area.

The trail now narrows and progressively becomes more of a true woods trail. A lengthy descent through occasionally draining areas of minor wetness is quite pleasant. Yellow trail markers become more evident. At 3.0 mi. (4.9 km) you skirt a beaver flooded area with an interesting low, winding dam. The trail splits at one point, but the parts soon merge again.

Mature beech, maple, yellow birch, and a few red spruce make up the forest through which you are now traveling. This region was not logged as recently as the land you saw earlier. As a result, it is more nearly a climax forest typical of this elevation.

The gradual descent goes on with a few knolls to change the pace. The outlet of Deep Lake and Twin Lakes is crossed in two parts at 3.6 mi. (5.8 km). The first part is hopped on rocks. Once over a small knoll, you cross the second part on a log bridge and turn left.

An easy grade takes you gradually up to a col. The trail is very comfortable here. From the top, a gradual descent takes you downward until, at 4.5 mi. (7.3 km), you pass some rock outcrops to your left. Then, a moderately steep grade takes you another 0.1 mi. (0.2 km) downward. Brooktrout Lake can be seen through the trees, but you will swing to the left and circle the northeast side of the lake several meters upslope from the shoreline.

Frequent ups and downs occur as you walk along with the lake in view. At 5.1 mi. (8.3 km) an informal campsite is passed, and the side trail to the lean-to is reached at 5.2 mi. (8.4 km).

The lean-to is located 25 yds. (23 m) off the trail to the right. It faces a large sheared-off boulder against which a fireplace is constructed. It makes a perfect heat reflector on cold, chilly nights. The lake is reached by a short path through dense spruces at the rear of the lean-to. The rock-lined shore is attractive, and the shallow water invites swimming. You are looking due west. A disappearing sun in late evening will provide the mood for a long campfire before turning in at night.

A path at the far end of the small lean-to clearing leads back to the main trail. It is another 0.7 mi. (1.1 km) of flat trail to the informal campsite on the shore of West Lake, and still another 1.8 mi. (2.9 km) along the shoreline to the former ranger station site clearing and two lean-tos at the west end of the lake.

Spruce Lake

Difficulty: Moderate, but a long trip
Round Trip Distance: 21.7 mi. (35.2 km)
Time Necessary: 2 days
Maps: Piseco Lake 15' Series, West Canada Lakes 15' Series,
      Piseco Lake metric

You have to walk a little to get to Spruce Lake, but it's worth the effort. This high elevation (2378 ft. [727 m]) lake provides a true wilderness experience. The trail you follow is part of the Northville-Placid Trail. From Piseco it is 38 mi. (61.6 km) through the West Canada Lakes Wilderness Area before a road is reached at Wakely Dam.

Access is off Rte. 8 in the village of Piseco. At the north end of the village, just west of the small airport, is a DEC signpost at a road junction. Following the road 0.8 mi. (1.3 km) north from this junction, you will find a parking area on the right. This is as far as vehicles should travel on this road.

From the parking area (0.0 mi.) the trail continues across the bridge over Cold Stream to private land. The route leaves the road and enters the woods. Following blue trail markers on a tote road through hardwood forest, you reach a cable barrier at 0.1 mi. (0.2 km). At 1.0 mi. (1.6 km) this flat route passes over a brook. Heading north, you cross a second brook at 2.0 mi. (3.9 km), after which rises and small pitches take you overland to a third brook at 2.4 mi. (3.9 km).

Swinging northwestward, a moderately steep slope soon begins. After gaining 180 ft. (55 m) in elevation, the trail again levels off, crosses several small brooks, and maintains its elevation at about 2000 ft. (612 m).

Descending slightly, you observe a PBM 1962 ft. (600 m) some 140 yds. (128 m) before the Fall Stream crossing. A small bridge takes you over Fall Stream, where a nice informal campsite is located. You may find bits and pieces of a heavy-gauge aluminum food storage container, strewn about and left by a bear many years ago. Fall Stream is at the 4.4 mi. (7.1 km) point and makes a good place for a rest break before the real exercise begins.

After following the left bank of the stream for about 150 yds. (138 m), the trail curves westward from the stream and begins a steady climb up a moderate grade. It levels off at 5.5 mi. (8.9 km). Now heading northwest, you descend an easy grade to a clearing at 5.9 mi. (9.6 km).

Crossing a small brook in the clearing, the trail passes a private camp that is on the right. Steady but gradual climbing takes you to the end of the clearing at 6.2 mi. (10.0 km). Soon after, the trail drops at a moderately steep rate and crosses the end of a vlei. From here you can see the remains of an old lumber camp, sitting on a hillside at the opposite side of the vlei. If time is not pressing, this might be an interesting side trip. As you continue your steady descent, you will see a side road to the right that leads generally in its direction.

At 6.8 mi. (11.0 km) the Jessup River is crossed on stones. This region is frequently lumbered, and you may see evidence of current work.

Swinging to the right and again heading north, you follow an old lumber road. Part way up a moderate grade, the route makes a left turn off the road at 7.0 mi. (11.3 km) and, pitching sharply up a steep little slope, soon rejoins the lumber road.

Still climbing, you approach a major logging road near top of grade. The N-P Trail swings left just before reaching it onto another tote road at 7.2 mi. (11.7 km). You continue the gradual climb for a while before the route finally levels. The trail enters another tote road as a trailing switch on the right at 7.5 mi. (12.2 km). A sign points the correct way.

A slight descent occurs before another junction with an arrow sign. (An old logging road comes in from the R; be careful not to take this on the return trip.) The way is now nearly level and several boardwalks help you to cross this wet area. Bloodgood Brook is crossed at 8.0 mi. and still more wet area is negotiated. A gradually climbing trail then begins to take you to drier ground, and a side trail at 9.5 mi. (15.4 km) leads left to the first Spruce Lake lean-to. This is a replacement lean-to. The site of the original lean-to is 200 ft. (61 m) farther along the side trail at the lake shore.

The trail continues along the east shore of Spruce Lake to a second trail junction at 10.3 mi. (16.7 km). Here, a side trail to the left leads down a moderate slope to another lean-to, tucked into a tiny clearing. Though this is not as pleasant a lean-to as the first, the swimming is excellent here.

Further along the shoreline, the N-P Trail crosses the wide, rocky outlet of Balsam Lake. Thirty-five yds. (32 m) beyond, a third trail junction is reached at 10.8 mi. (17.5 km). A path to the left takes you to the third and most attractive of the Spruce Lake lean-tos. Set back in the trees a short distance, this is the most private of the three, but since it is furthest along the trail it is the least used. Just before reaching the lean-to, you pass a grassy clearing.

Spruce Lake is a beautiful place. Loons still call in the night with piercing screams that bring you out of a sound sleep into instant alertness. Otter families can be seen playing in the water and cruising up and down the lake. It is a hard place to leave, unless you are heading farther into this wilderness area.

Sucker Brook Trail

Difficulty: Moderately challenging
Round Trip Distance: 13.8 mi. (22.4 km)
Time Necessary: 2 days
Map: ADK Central Region map; Lewey Mountain 7.5'; Indian Lake and
    Wakely Mountain metrics; Indian Lake 15'

The Sucker Brook Trail exemplifies a type of backpacking opportunity in the Adirondacks that all too often is overlooked. Most hikers want to climb a mountain or camp on the shore of a distant lake. Consequently, on reaching their destination they almost always meet others who had the same idea. Yet, on almost any map quadrangle of the Adirondacks, one can find trails that seem to head off into nowhere. Many a backpacker has spent countless hours of pleasure poring over maps and planning trips to such places. Finding good fishing spots, old mines, abandoned lumber camps, or even old survey points may be the ostensible reasons for such outings. When it comes right down to the nub of the matter, however, it's just plain fun to head into an area where the route isn't four feet wide with a bridge over every tiny brook. It's challenging to have to figure out for yourself how to get past a beaver bog or across a stream, and not knowing exactly where you will set up camp at night adds a little excitement to the trip.

Once you get used to the idea of seeking out-of-the-way locations, you'll find there's a great deal of space in the Adirondacks where you can be alone. Eventually, bushwhacking trips may be your style. Real skill and woods savvy are needed for such experiences, but there's a certain sense of wilderness that can only be achieved by going it on your own.

The first part of the Sucker Brook Trail is well used by day hikers from Lewey Lake Public Campsite, and you follow a well maintained trail as far as the col between Cellar and Lewey mountains. From the col, though, the route is a wilderness path where one can feel a real sense of isolation. In recent years the remainder of the trail has been better maintained than in the past, but the contrast with the first part of the trail is still noticeable. As you head into the West Canada Lakes Wilderness Area, you will need to be resourceful to reach your goal. That's what makes it so enjoyable.

Access to the trailhead is on the north side of the bridge over the outlet of Lewey Lake. This is on Rte. 30 between Indian Lake and Speculator. Here, a macadam road leads west into tenting areas of the campsite. While it is possible to leave your vehicle at the roadside, it would be safer to leave it at the boat launching site nearby or at the campsite parking area, which is approximately 0.2 mi. (0.3 km) south of the bridge.

From Rte. 30, walk a short distance along the macadam road to a small clearing on the right. Here a sign (0.0 mi.) marks the official beginning of the trail. It is possible to remain on the macadam road, bearing right at a fork, to its end. You then hike up a grade past a gate to the right, where the trail is intersected.

The trail heads westward through hardwood forest. Gradually you realize that you are gaining elevation. The way is quite enjoyable. Occasionally, Sucker Brook is heard below you to the left, but it is seldom seen.

A large tributary stream is crossed at 1.3 mi. (2.1 km), and a steady grade takes you upward to the 2.3 mi. (3.7 km) point, where the trail levels and follows the contour of the land for awhile.

At 2.7 mi. (4.4 km) the trail markedly steepens. The next 0.3 mi. (0.5 km) is a steep climb to the col between Cellar and Lewey mountains. From the col it is a relatively easy bushwhack to the summit of Lewey Mountain. Cellar Mountain's summit is a much stiffer climb through considerable blowdown.

The col is pleasantly level, with ferns and a white pine grove as a change of scenery. As the trail starts the descent towards Colvin Brook, it is readily apparent that fewer people travel this section. Well marked, the route narrows considerably. This is a true wilderness trail, and a sense of the wild presses in on you as you go along.

At 4.6 mi. (7.5 km) Colvin Brook is reached; you will cross and recross this stream ten times before you leave it. Take care, since the rocks are slippery. In springtime it can be hazardous. You weave your way along the stream for about an hour, keeping a sharp eye out for trail markers.

A lean-to is reached at 6.9 mi. (11.2 km), where it sits in a picturesque spot along the Cedar River. The Cedar River is broad and shallow here. The crossing is slightly downstream from the lean-to and can be a bit tricky. If you plan to cross, plan your sequence of rock hops well or you may take a dunking.

The Sucker Brook Trail continues another 1.0 mi. (1.6 km) on a level course to a trail junction with the Northville–Placid Trail. This is just east of Lamphere Ridge.

Take your time on this trip. It has a few spots where rushing can result in problems, but if you want the flavor of real wilderness, this is a fine outing.

Cedar Lake

6. The Black River Wild Forest Area

The late 1700s saw Nat Foster and Jonathan "Jock" Wright running their traplines through these woods, just as Roscoe and Bert Conkling would do in later years. Lumbermen came as early as 1866, when Phil McGuire of Punkeytown (Forestport) cut down trees to provide spars for Yankee and British shipbuilders. Rev. A. L. Byron-Curtiss led an influx of "city sports" to this area when he began summering at North Lake in 1892.

Canal builders started pressing for a "forest preserve" when the headwaters of the Black River and its canal began to close off due to the flooding and drought effects of the then current lumbering practices. Some people, seeing what was coming, bought up huge acreage for private clubs before the state could create the Forest Preserve. The Adirondack League Club, Lookout Mountain Club, and the Bisby Club were a few of the major organizations to form in this region.

The Forest Preserve was created, but lumbering still continued on private lands well into the 20th century. The last great logging river run in the Adirondacks occurred on the Moose River when the McKeever crib dam broke on June 3, 1947, sending thousands of logs downriver. You can still see the remains of the dam as you cross the Rte. 28 bridge over the Moose River at McKeever.

Today, this area has 30 miles of trails and 36 bodies of water. The winter brings a few trappers and many snowmobilers into this country, but in summer only a few anglers and hikers venture off the beaten paths. Chub, Gull, Woodhull, Sand, and Nicks lakes are but a few of the places backpackers can go for interesting outings.

Big Woodhull and Bear Lakes Loop

Difficulty: Easy, with a few moderate grades
Round Trip Distance: 9.3 mi. (15.1 km)
Time Necessary: 2 days
Map: McKeever 15' Series, McKeever metric

Topographic maps refer to it as Woodhull Lake, but DEC trail signs call it Big Woodhull to prevent its being confused with Little Woodhull Lake a few miles to the south. The hiker will find a variety of trail types on this outing. The first part of the hike follows the old road to Woodhull Lake. The state made it into a fire truck road, so it is quite good as far as the Remsen Falls junction. From there on, it is an unimproved snowmobile trail. In contrast, the return trip via Bear Lake is a marvelous woods trail of more recent construction. Bear Lake, unless affected by beaver activity, is completely surrounded by sandy beach.

Access to the trailhead is off Rte. 28 at McKeever. The turnoff is to the east, a little over a mile north of Otter Lake Village. A state road sign indicates the hamlet of McKeever on the south side of Moose River. Drive along the old macadam road 0.2 mi. (0.3 km) from Rte. 28. At a curve in the road bear right onto a gravel road, pass the old railroad station, and cross the railroad tracks a short distance further along the way. Proceed along a level dirt road 0.4 mi. (0.6 km) to a large DEC snowmobile parking area. The snowmobile trail forks to the right, but you should continue driving on the left fork past the parking area. Another 0.1 mi. (0.2 km) of driving will bring you to a second parking area and DEC trail register for the hiking route.

DAY 1. The truck trail heads east from the gate (0.0 mi.) at the end of the parking area. Rarely seen red trail markers guide you along an almost flat sandy trail. Closed to vehicles except in emergency, this trail makes a nice cross-country ski trail in the winter. The lane in summer is grassy and the walk enjoyably easy. (At 0.9 mi. [1.5 km], a DEC trail sign indicates that a side trail to the right follows blue trail markers to Bear Lake. Continue straight ahead on the truck road.)

Ferns and moss-covered boulders are numerous. Three clearings are passed. Two have brooks running through them. Willows and black spruces surround the openings in the forest.

A four-way trail junction is reached at 2.8 mi. (4.5 km), about an hour after you begin the hike. (To the left, the trail leads 0.5 mi. [0.8 km] to the South Branch of the Moose River, where Remson Falls is found. A lean-to is 0.2 mi. [0.3 km] downstream, but on the far shore. The river is very difficult to cross at this point.) The trail straight ahead at this junction leads another 3.2 mi. (5.2 km) to a junction, where a side trail right takes you 2.5 mi. (4.1 km) to the summit of Woodhull Mountain. Open views are difficult to locate.

Turn right and follow blue trail markers up a moderate grade. This section of road is less used and more narrow. At 3.0 mi. (4.9 km), an extended wire cable crosses the road and weaves through the woods on each side for several meters. Thirty yards (28 m) beyond, the snowmobile trail from McKeever enters from the right front.

Turn left at this acute junction and head down a curving grade along the snowmobile route. A difference between Wild Forest and Wilderness designated Forest Preserve land is immediately obvious. In the Wilderness Area no vehicular traffic is permitted. On some Wild Forest roads, however, where there has been a historic record of vehicular use before land designation was assigned, vehicles are still permitted. Such seems to be the case here. Hunters have used vehicles, and in some steep areas their tires have gouged out ruts.

The grade ranges from gradual to moderate. In the next 1.3 mi. (2.1 km), 340 ft. (104 m) elevation will be gained. The trail levels periodically, and in one of these level zones, on the right at approximately 4.0 mi. (6.5 km),

Black River Wild Forest Area

there is a large hunters' campsite. Height of land is reached at 4.3 mi. (7.0 km). An unmarked trail junction is located here. The road straight ahead leads 0.2 mi. (0.3 km) down to Wolf Landing on Big Woodhull Lake.

Turn right at this junction. As you begin a swing around the west shore of Big Woodhull Lake, elevation is gradually lost. You can catch glimpses of the lake to the left.

The woods trail from Bear Lake enters from the right at 4.6 mi. (7.5 km). A few meters further on you cross the outlet of Bloodsucker Brook. Immediately there is another trail junction. The right fork, with blue markers, is the snowmobile trail to Sand Lake and Woodgate. Turn left here and follow red trail markers along a woods path. Big Woodhull Lake and its lean-to are reached at 4.8 mi. (7.8 km).

This large body of water has rock along much of its shoreline and is most appealing. If the lean-to is not the largest in the Adirondack Park, it must run a close second. This incredible structure has a double fireplace and will easily hold 20 people. Unfortunately, numerous trees have been cut down around it.

DAY 2. From the lean-to (0.0 mi.), return 0.2 mi. (0.3 km) to the Bear Lake trail junction beside Bloodsucker Brook.

Turn left and follow yellow trail markers up the left side of Bloodsucker Brook. At 0.3 mi. (0.5 km) a well-built beaver dam is passed, and soon thereafter Bloodsucker Pond appears to the left front. In spite of its name, this is a most attractive sheet of water. Blueberry bushes form a necklace around this hidden jewel in the forest, and beaver meadows surround it.

The path heads to the north across rolling terrain. The fern-covered forest floor is lush and very comfortable to walk on. After about ten minutes of walking, the path swings to the west and begins the long, gentle decline to Bear Lake.

A large inlet of Bear Lake is approached at 1.6 mi. (2.6 km). Follow this to the lake. After ten minutes of walking you find yourself high above the stream; then you drop rapidly downward as you reach Bear Lake at 2.0 mi. (3.2 km).

Several good but informal campsites are found where the inlet enters the lake. A blue-marked DEC trail intersects from the right and continues southward to the Bear Creek parking area at Woodgate. The lake sits in a basin, surrounded by a high horseshoe-shaped ridge on its northern end. The southern end opens up, and from its outlet Bear Creek drains through miles of wetlands. The shore is entirely lined by a fine gravel and sand beach that invites swimming. The presence of such an alluring lake here is somehow unexpected, and one is tempted to stay here and camp.

You cross the inlet and follow the blue-marked trail around the eastern shoreline, heading northward. Fifty yards (46 m) after crossing another inlet at the north end of the lake on a log bridge, the trail makes an abrupt turn to the right. From here it mounts a moderate grade, winding up through a narrow gorge. At 2.4 mi. (3.9 km) water pirouettes off a high cliff, gliding downward to join the brook you have been following. Soon after, height of land is reached and you proceed on level ground for a few minutes. You then begin a long gradual descent to the McKeever truck trail.

A stream is crossed several times. At 3.2 mi. (5.2 km) a short side trail to the left leads to a small shelter under a large boulder, just off the trail. From this point you descend a brief moderate grade and negotiate a flat wet section. The muddy, rutted, snowmobile trail is crossed at 3.4 mi. (5.8 km). Continue to follow along the left side of the brook. The truck trail is reached at 3.6 mi. (5.8 km).

Turn left and return 0.9 mi. (1.5 km) to the McKeever parking area. This is reached at 4.5 mi. (7.3 km).

Sand Lake Falls

Difficulty: Easy, but watch where you're going
Round Trip Distance: 13.4 mi. (21.7 km)
Time Necessary: 2 days
Map: McKeever 15' Series, McKeever metric

This trip takes you to an isolated lean-to by a broad waterfall with dozens of deep coldwater trout holes in the cascades below it. Not far away, a wide stillwater extends for a great distance through protected forest. A network of old logging roads is followed: some are still used by vehicles, others are grassy lanes, and some may need brushing out. Trail markers are well posted where needed and absent when the way is obvious. Be alert to changes in direction at numerous intersections.

Access to the trailhead is off Rte. 28 at Woodgate. Turn east onto Bear Creek Road at the blinker light. Proceed along this road as far as you can travel. Railroad tracks are passed at 0.8 mi. (1.3 km). You reach the DEC Bear Creek parking area and trail register at 3.2 mi. (5.2 km).

The trail leaves the parking area, running northeastward along Woodhull Rd., now a snowmobile trail. A blue-marked trail on the right (which goes to Chub and Gull ponds) is passed at 0.25 mi. (0.4 km). At a junction at 0.4 mi. (0.6 km), take the left turn past a barricade to avoid further muddy trail. This yellow-marked grassy old woods road provides much more enjoyable walking.

Heading north down a gradual descent, the trail soon levels. When you reach still another fork, at 1.3 mi. (2.1 km), bear right. (The left fork goes on another 50 yds [46 m] to Bear Creek.) The nearly level route is only occasionally marred by ruts of ATVs.

After crossing two small brooks, you see a red-marked trail at right, heading uphill at 1.9 mi. (3.1 km). This is the Gull Pond Trail. Continuing along the flat yellow trail, you reach the Bear Lake junction at 2.5 mi. (4.1 km). It branches north while the Sand Lake Falls Trail swings to the southeast.

Woodhull Rd. is rejoined at 2.8 mi. (4.5 km). Bear left and continue northward. Muddy trail is left behind as the route climbs steadily but easily to drier and more level ground. At 3.6 mi. (5.8 km), a major junction is reached. The Sand Lake Falls trail bears right, now following blue trail markers. Easy to miss, this turnoff occurs before you reach buildings and just before the comical Millbrook sign. (If still standing, it reads "Village of Millbrook, population 0 [Dry town]". The yellow-marked trail forks left through "Millbrook" and another 3.7 mi. [6.0 km] to the lean-to at Woodhull Lake.)

The remaining portion of the trip passes along a snowmobile route that doesn't appear to have been used for several years (1995). In a few places the undergrowth is closing in on the sides of the trail, but trail markers are very well posted and the majority of the route is easily followed. The worst part is the first 200 yds. (183 km) from this junction.

Turn right and follow blue trail markers from the trail signs. Yellow snowmobile markers are also posted along the way. The trail passes through a short zone of blowdown and heavy undergrowth; you are in a small gully and the correct way follows it, curving to the right in a gradual arc. You soon cross a hunter's trail. Avoid it, and avoid a second hunter's trail that enters from the left a shorter distance along the way. A small opening with branching logging roads is soon reached. A trail sign points to the correct route, which crosses a branch of Mill Brook on a wooden bridge. Bearing left, the route becomes quite easy to follow.

You walk generally eastward with little change in grade and reach a large clearing at 4.3 mi. (7.0 km). Apple trees and various pieces of old implements give evidence that someone once called this place home. Nature is reclaiming it as small spruce invade, but it still is an interesting place to poke around and try to imagine who may have lived here more than 50 years ago.

The route sidles along the right side of the clearing and returns to the woods at the east corner of the old homestead. A wet stretch is passed before a gradual increase in elevation begins. The route is generally east. Gentle grades continue to 5.8 mi. (9.4 km), where direction of travel becomes increasingly to the southeast. A descent begins. Several small brooks are crossed as you drop down into the Woodhull Creek valley.

A junction for a trail is reached at 5.9 mi. (9.6 km); you may miss it on the way in, but it can easily be taken on the way out. Blue arrows are painted on a beech tree. (This trail turns left and heads generally northeast in the direction of the trail from Sand Lake to North Lake, which it probably joins. It has no DEC markers but follows tree blazes, which are painted blue. A hunter's camp and well constructed garbage pit are a short distance along this trail.) Remember to bear left at this junction on the return trip and head northwest.

You continue to descend the open trail. The sounds of rushing water are heard long before the charging stream comes into sight. The first indication of the lean-to is when its glittering wood shingle roof catches your eye. The trail swings around to the front of the lean-to and enters a very large clearing where a small but excellent lean-to faces Woodhull Creek at 6.7 mi. (10.9 km).

The lean-to sits well back from the top of Sand Lake Falls. Perhaps 35 yds. (32 m) of clearing separate the shelter from the wide stream. Sand Lake Falls is wide but not especially high. It tumbles from one deep pool to another for hundreds of meters downstream as it slices its way through Adirondack bedrock.

It is hard to imagine what this great rushing stream is doing here until one studies several maps. Big Woodhull Lake drains into Sand Lake. Sand Lake and all four lakes of the Bisby Chain drain into Woodhull Creek. Consequently, the waters of six lakes plunge over Sand Lake Falls. Temporarily held in a stillwater over a kilometer long above the falls, the water shoots into the wide gorge. Gravity pulls it ever onward to Chub Pond, Kayuta Lake at Forestport, and finally to the Black River. Such a spectacle in this isolated forest is like an oasis in the desert.

The snowmobile trail heads out of the far side of the clearing. It parallels the stream but is not in sight of it. The great, wide stillwater is 0.2 mi. (0.3 km) beyond the lean-to and should be visited. Though the snowmobile trail ends at the shore of the stillwater, deer trails provide easy routes along its edge for quite a distance. (The snowmobile trail crosses the water and continues another 3.9 mi. [6.3 km] to North Lake Rd.) All manner of waterfowl can be seen on this protected waterway, where the deer seem genuinely surprised to see a human.

Woodhull Lake Lean-to

Ha-De-Ron-Dah Wilderness Area

7. The Ha-De-Ron-Dah Wilderness Area

The Ha-de-ron-dah Wilderness Area is a 26,600-acre forest on the west side of Rte. 28, generally south and west of Old Forge. In this section of the Adirondacks, one usually thinks of the three branches of the Moose River. Though the outflow of the 59 bodies of water of the Ha-de-ron-dah eventually joins the Moose River near Lyonsdale, a separate watershed actually exists. All of the lakes and ponds mentioned in this section drain generally westward into Pine Creek and then on to the Moose and Black rivers.

Within the area's forest is a considerable variety of floral associations. The southern half has had significant fire damage in the past, which was severe enough to affect the soils. As the earth rebuilds its fertility, numerous bracken fern, berry bushes, pin cherry, and aspen are seen. North of the Big Otter Lake truck trail, on the other hand, pines up to 40 inches in diameter can be found. In between, a hardwood forest of yellow birch, beech, and maple grows. Low areas have wetlands and beaver meadows.

Less than a 1000 ft. (306 m) change in elevation is found in this region, and no more than a 250 ft. (76 m) change is found on the trails described here. In general, long easy routes with occasional short ups and downs typify this rolling terrain.

The Civilian Conservation Corps (CCC) built the Big Otter Lake truck trail in the 1930s to permit quicker reaction to forest fires. It's still usable for that purpose today, but it is becoming a grassy lane where walking is most enjoyable. The large old stone fireplace just before the gate at Thendara is all that is left of the CCC camp that once occupied the open meadow here. A snowmobile club is planning to incorporate the fireplace into part of a building addition to their clubhouse. It is fitting that fires should once again burn in this historic structure.

The six lean-tos of this region and many of the 27.3 mi. (44.2 km) of foot trails are seldom used. Few people seem to know the area well. Those who do tend to come back to it year after year. It is good hiking country.

Middle Branch Lake via the Big Otter Lake Truck Trail

Difficulty: Easy and relaxing
Round Trip Distance: 11.8 mi. (19.1 km)
Time Necessary: 2 days
Map: McKeever 15' Series, Thendara metric

This outing takes you over very gentle trails to a nice little lake. It is one of the better beginner hikes because there are no major grades. The larger portion of the trip is along the Big Otter Lake truck trail. This old road is slowly growing in and is quite pleasant to travel. The last mile to the lean-to is a true woods trail and makes a nice variation. By using the Cedar Pond crossover trail, both hikes described here can be combined to make a much longer outing possible.

Access to the trailhead is off Rte. 28, south of Old Forge and Thendara. Immediately south of the railroad underpass at Thendara a gravel road turns north. There is no sign, but the road leads 0.4 mi. (0.6 km) to a parking area and road barrier. In the winter, both a snowmobile trail and the excellent cross-country ski trail along the Big Otter Lake truck trail originate at this point. (They soon split.) In the summer, only an early morning deer is seen here.

From the DEC register and road barrier (0.0 mi.), the route follows blue trail markers up a short moderate grade. At 0.1 mi. (0.2 km) the snowmobile trail splits to the right and the hiking trail continues along the road. Another, more effective, vehicle barrier is seen at 0.4 mi. (0.6 km). A short, moderate grade past the barrier soon becomes a long, gradual stroll downward before it levels off near Indian Brook. Glimpses of beaver houses are seen across the meadows through the trees. A flat, wide sandy stretch takes you across the Indian Brook flood plain at 1.0 mi. (1.6 km). Insects and birds of every description are found here.

The trail gains slight elevation and the way becomes wooded again as you come off the flood plain. At 1.5 mi. (2.4 km) a trail junction is reached where the East Pond trail branches to the right. Tents are needed for camping at East Pond since the lean-to burned down.

The road from the junction begins a steady incline, making the Moose River Mountain trail junction seem farther than it really is from the East Pond trail junction. This junction is located near height of land at the 2.2 mi. (3.6 km) point; a widening of the trail and a Big Otter Lake distance sign mark the spot. The fire tower has been removed from the mountain, and the trail is no longer maintained. It leads another mile, and 200 ft. (61 m) of elevation are gained before the summit is reached.

From height of land the truck trail begins a stepped, easy decline of gradual grades. Occasional large beeches are seen. As they age, a fungus attacks them from within their cores, and they eventually become victims of strong winds and topple over. Examine the hollowed centers of these giants.

A major tributary running off Moose River Mountain crosses the trail in a spruce lowland at 3.7 mi. (6.0 km) on its way to the South Inlet of Big Otter Lake. An informal campsite is on the right of the trail. This is a good place for a rest.

Continuing on easy trail, another short moderate decline brings you to the Middle Branch Lake trail junction at 4.9 mi. (7.9 km). A sign indicates you should turn left and follow yellow trail markers. The route from here to the lake is over a forest path where footing must be closely watched. The change in trail type is welcome, however. The course is generally to the south through a young forest of smaller trees.

Another junction is found at 5.6 mi. (9.1 km). Here, the crossover trail to Cedar Pond forks to the left. It is 0.9 mi. (1.5 km) of moderately tough trail over two ridges.

Middle Branch Lake is straight ahead on a red-marked trail. The vegetation again changes as you pass through an old burn area. Many bracken fern and a more open woods greet you. You pass a large pyramidal boulder just before you reach the lean-to at 5.9 mi. (9.6 km).

The lean-to sits above the water on a small point overlooking the lake. Your view from the midpoint of the eastern shoreline is to the southwest. A few informal campsites are near the lean-to, and fishermen have made paths along the shore of the lake.

Middle Settlement Lake via the Scusa Access Trail

Difficulty: Easy to moderate
Round Trip Distance: 7.8 mi. (12.6 km)
Time Necessary: 2 days
Map: McKeever 15' Series, Thendara metric

This loop route leads to what many feel is the nicest lean-to in the Ha-de-ron-dah Wilderness Area. It certainly has an attractive setting. Unfortunately, the trails leading to it are not as interesting as those in the more northern sections.

At the lake is an interesting cave, a lookout ledge to climb, and a large beaver dam. This lean-to is frequently used by snowshoers for winter camping.

Access to the trailhead is from a large parking area with picnic tables just south of the Okara Lakes. This is on the southeast side of Rte. 28 approximately 2.9 mi. (4.7 km) south of the railroad underpass at Thendara, near Old Forge. The trailhead begins on private land across the road from the north end of this parking area. A sign indicates the way to state land.

DAY 1. The trail leading to state land is called the Scusa Access Trail. From Rte. 28 (0.0 mi.) cross the wooden bridge over the small outlet of the Okara Lakes to where a DEC trail register and trail signs are located. Follow red trail markers.

The hardest part of the trip now leads up a moderately steep slope 0.1 mi. (0.2 km) to a bare rock opening. Imbedded in this rocky ridge are both milky and rose quartz. The trail then gradually loses elevation, crossing two small brooks on log walks before regaining some of the lost elevation.

The trail junction with the Brown Tract Trail is reached at 0.6 mi. (1.0 km). Middle Settlement Lake can be reached by traveling in either direction from this junction, but the lay of the land is such that a counterclockwise loop is preferable. It is therefore recommended that you turn to the right (northeastward).

Turning right, follow both yellow and red trail markers. Avoid the unmarked trail you will soon see to your right. Approximately 100 ft. (31 m) further on, at 0.8 mi. (1.3 km), another junction is reached.

Your trail turns sharply left here and continues to follow red markers. (The Brown Tract Trail continues straight ahead 2.5 mi. [4.1 km] to the Okara Lakes parking area.)

A few minutes along the Cedar Pond Trail a wet area is crossed on an unusually long log walk. Immediately thereafter a junction is reached, just before a moderate grade begins. A few meters to the right are some trail signs, and the uphill trail from those signs soon merges with the red-marked trail you have been following. The grade levels and then continues over rolling terrain. Some 10 minutes later a moderate grade takes you down to a small brook. On the opposite side of the brook at 1.1 mi. (1.8 km) is another trail junction. The yellow-marked trail to the right leads 0.5 mi. (0.8 km) north to a campsite beside Grass Pond.

Bear left and continue to follow red trail markers. You walk on the level for awhile before beginning a gradual decline to the crossing of the Grass Pond outlet at 1.7 mi. (2.8 km). This large rushing stream is a good place to get a drink and rest. If you look downstream, you can see the beginning of an unnamed pond from which this outflow of Grass Pond continues on to Cedar Pond.

Beyond the outlet, you climb a few meters away from the water to drier ground. Then, heading downstream, you parallel the stream. Generally keeping to the contour, you drop into occasional dips as small brooks are crossed. You begin a gradual descent at 2.3 mi. (3.7 km) and can see Cedar Pond through the trees to your left front. The trail swings along the north side of Cedar Pond but is well back from the shoreline.

Fifteen minutes later two small, shallow, clear-flowing creeks are crossed. The far bank of the second one is steep. The trail follows a hummock ridge through spruce and soon passes a spring (condition not known). At 3.0 mi. (4.8 km), the site of the former Cedar Pond lean-to is passed.

Most hikers won't be impressed with the marshy wetlands of the almost filled-in north end of Cedar Pond. Its water is murky when you can find it. Botanists, however, may wish to spend a whole weekend here because of the great variety of water plants available for study. Black spruces form a nice background setting, and there are abundant blueberry bushes on the marshland. It is an interesting ecosystem.

At the left rear of the lean-to is the junction of three trails. The crossover trail to Middle Branch Lake heads to the right in a generally northward direction and follows yellow trail markers 1.2 mi. (1.9 km) over a pair of moderately steep ridges to the lean-to on Middle Branch Lake. The trail you should follow is the Middle Settlement Lake trail to the left, which also follows yellow trail markers but heads to the south.

The trail is a soft woods path. Some elevation is gained and the wetlands of Cedar Pond can be seen in the distance to your left. At 3.4 mi. (5.5 km), the trail makes an abrupt left-hand turn, drops down, and crosses the outlet of Cedar Pond on a log bridge. A swampy area is crossed with little difficulty before minor elevation is gained and you reach drier ground. To the right the ground begins to rise sharply, and finally you reach rock cliffs with boulders at their base.

An immense boulder is passed on the left at 4.0 mi. (6.5 km). Just past it, on the right, is a smaller boulder, which has a small cave under it. Rocks have been used to fill in open spots around its entrance. At one time a wooden bed was inside, and winter campers have been known to sleep there.

A small creek is crossed 70 yds. (64 m) beyond the huge boulder. The Middle Settlement Lake Access Trail junction comes in from the left, on the far side of the creek. Turning right, and after traveling a few more meters, you reach the shallow silted end of Middle Settlement Lake.

The trail bears right, along the north shore of the lake. It soon comes very close to the shore at a grassy spot. Immediately afterward, a junction is reached. A large sign is located here, but the whole junction can be missed if you are gazing out at the lake, which has become increasingly more attractive. This red-marked side trail leads 0.2 mi. (0.3 km) to a rocky ledge some 150 ft. (46 m) above the lake surface. From the ledge you can get a fairly good view of the surrounding country. You may wish to make the climb after depositing your pack at the lean-to.

As the trail moves a little farther back from the shore, you pass an informal campsite before reaching the lean-to at 4.5 mi. (7.3 km).

The lean-to is about two-thirds of the way down the lake and sits about 10 ft. (3 m) above the water on a large rock outcrop. The view is marvelous, and the changes in light intensity on the far shore as the sun drops behind you at sunset are a delight to behold. Deep water beyond the rock outcrop invites you to a refreshing swim.

There are two informal campsites farther along the trail past the lean-to. You should walk down the trail to the lake outlet, where there is a wide beaver dam over 6 ft. (2 m) high.

DAY 2. You could make a longer loop than the one described here by continuing southwestward on this trail beyond the lake outlet until it connects up with the Brown Tract Trail again. This would make the return trip 5.7 mi. (9.2 km) instead of the 3.3 mi. (5.3 km) trip described here. However, you should be prepared to wade through waist-deep water when crossing Middle Settlement Creek.

The suggested return trip retraces the trail 0.5 mi. (0.8 km) back to the aforementioned trail junction with the Middle Settlement Lake Access Trail.

The blue-marked trail has mostly gradual grades with some minor ups and downs as streams are crossed. A small ridge and then two wet areas are crossed. Both have log walks. From the second one, at 1.4 mi. (2.3 km), you can see the same unnamed wetland pond to the left that you saw yesterday from the opposite side when you crossed the outlet of Grass Pond.

A gentle upgrade takes you through a section of raspberries and ferns to the trail junction with the Brown Tract Trail at 1.7 mi. (2.8 km). Turn left here and follow yellow trail markers. The character of the forest rapidly changes to more mature hardwoods as you reach higher ground. The grades are so gradual that height of land is barely noticed at 2.2 mi. (3.6 km). A gradual, almost flat, trail takes you downward. Finally, after a last moderate drop to a stream crossing, you reach the Scusa Access Trail junction at 2.7 mi. (4.4 km).

Turn right and follow red trail markers 0.6 mi. (1.0 km) to Rte. 28, reached at 3.3 mi. (5.3 km).

For additional trips in this area and the following, refer to *Guide to Adirondack Trails: West-Central Region* (ADK).

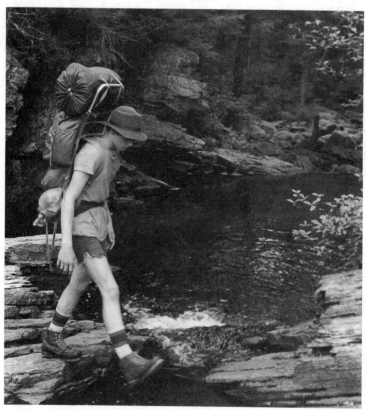

8. The Pigeon Lake Wilderness Area

The Pigeon Lake Wilderness Area extends from Stillwater Reservoir to Raquette Lake. Together with the Five Ponds Wilderness Area and the Nehasane Area, acquired in 1979, it forms an immense block of wilderness in which relatively few foot trails exist. Often it has been the backpacking skier, in the dead of winter, who has penetrated this land. A small network of trails does exist, however.

In 1876 Jim Higby built a rough bark shanty for William Dutton on the North Shore of Big Moose Lake, and in 1878 Jack Sheppard built a permanent camp for some New York sportsmen. Other camps appeared in the region, but the difficulty of access kept this country from ever becoming densely populated. Still, resorts were built. The sensational murder of Grace Brown by Chester Gillette on Big Moose Lake in 1906 drew temporary attention and was later chronicled by Theodore Dreiser in *An American Tragedy*.

Within the 50,800 acres of the Pigeon Lake Wilderness Area lie some 64 bodies of water. Only four lean-tos are found here and two of them must be reached by water. The backpacker will need a tent and be prepared to rough it, but the country is magnificent.

Anglers and hunters have made many woods trails. There is opportunity for a true wilderness experience in this region, and those with the necessary knowledge and skills will find the kind of country few realize still exists in the Adirondacks.

The two outings described here may be linked to make a longer trip. It is also possible to continue northeast from Constable Pond to Pigeon Lake and West Mountain. The trip into West Mountain is rough, and you must be prepared to get your feet wet, but it can be a great trip for the experienced backpacker.

For additional trips in this area refer to *Guide to Adirondack Trails: West-Central Region* (ADK).

Queer Lake via the Chain Ponds Loop

Difficulty: Easy to moderate
Round Trip Distance: 8.6 mi. (13.9 km)
Time Necessary: 2 days
Map: Big Moose 15' Series, Eagle Bay metric

Few outings give you the sense of wilderness as quickly as this one. Though reasonably close to a public highway, only a few fishermen and hunters head back into this country. The majority of them head directly for Queer

Lake from Windfall Pond; thus, the Chain Ponds Loop is still wild and primitive. The trail is a true woodspath, not a wide thoroughfare, but it is well marked and for the most part in excellent condition. The only lean-to is found at Queer Lake, but all of the ponds have informal campsites. It is as a backpacking trail should be.

Trailhead access is from the DEC parking area on the Eagle Bay-Big Moose Road. This is 3.3 mi. (5.3 km) from Eagle Bay and about 1.9 mi. (3.1 km) north of the Moss Lake parking area. The small sign on the north side of the road easily can be missed if you're not looking for it. The parking area is quite large but hidden by trees.

Trail distances given in this section often are at variance with the posted trail signs seen on the trails.

DAY 1. From the DEC register (0.0 mi.), follow the yellow-marked trail east 0.2 mi. (0.3 km) to where it turns left and crosses a bridge. The trail straight ahead leads to an informal campsite.

Climb over two small knolls, and at 0.7 mi. (I.I km) recross the creek at a point where the water cascades through a small flume. The trail turns left and briefly parallels the creek to Beaver Meadow, then bears right and climbs beside Windfall Pond outlet to a trail junction at I.I mi. (1.8 km) at Windfall Pond. (The left fork trail leads 1.6 mi. (2.6 km) to Queer Lake's shore.)

Turning right from this junction, follow the blue-marked trail up a short moderate grade to the southeast. There is a nice view of Windfall Pond below to your left before you turn into the immense hardwood forest.

After 10 minutes on a true woods path, you approach a small col having a rocky wall covered with thick mosses. A gradual descent takes you to the edge of a large pond at 1.5 mi. (2.4 km).

Swinging left of the pond, you gradually ascend again and see more interesting rock formations on your left. These rock structures have considerable quartz in them. Small caves, cracks, and moss growths attract your attention. The trail follows a narrow gully which presses in on you.

At 2.4 mi. (3.9 km) you reach the Cascade Lake Link Trail at a junction. (The red-marked trail to the right leads 2.0 mi. (3.2 km) to Cascade Lake.)

Turn left here, still following the blue markers. Drop down and across the narrow gully floor you have been paralleling and cross it. Some ups and downs eventually become just downs, and you reach Chain Ponds at 2.9 mi. (4.7 km).

The trail crosses a brook which connects a vlei on your right to the most southern of the three Chain Ponds on the left. The clear waters and open woods make this an attractive location. The trail skirts the east shore after climbing a small incline. For several minutes, you drink in the beauty of the pond as you walk along. Finally, you veer away from the water and make a brief climb to a defile through the ridge at 3.2 mi. (5.2 km). This narrow pass has rugged cliffs rising to your right, with all manner of small conifers clinging to its sides. One gets the feeling of primeval forest.

Pigeon Lake Wilderness Area

Once through the defile a long descent begins, ending at a four-way trail junction at Queer Lake. This is reached at 3.8 mi. (6.2 km). A few meters to your right is Queer Lake. The Windfall Pond trail is to your left.

Straight ahead (northwest) is the trail you should follow to the lean-to. Cross the wet outlet of Queer Lake on a long log walk and follow the perimeter of the lake a short distance. The trail then makes an abrupt left-hand turn and climbs a moderate grade. Be sure you don't miss this turn and take the unmarked fishermen's path that continues along the lake shore.

Continue along your route to the Mays Pond trail junction at 4.2 mi. (6.8 km). Do not turn left onto the Mays Pond trail even though it has the same yellow trail markers you have been following since the last trail junction. Keep to the trail you have been on until a stand of hemlocks is reached at 4.5 mi. (7.3 km). Here, the yellow-marked Chub Pond trail turns left. Avoid it.

Instead, bear right and follow the red-marked trail down the grade to the lake shore. A log walk takes you across the soggy approach to the peninsula where the lean-to is situated. Follow the western edge of the peninsula to its narrow neck. Then cross over to the eastern side, where you'll quickly arrive at the lean-to at 4.8 mi. (7.8 km). Should you miss the crossover spot, you'll walk another five minutes before arriving at the end of the long peninsula.

Whoever built the Queer Lake lean-to knew how to do a proper job. Set in a grassy clearing, it catches breezes off the lake all day long. It has a good fireplace. Even the deacon's seat has a notch cut in it so you can easily sweep debris from the lean-to. An eaves trough keeps rain water from dripping in front of the lean-to.

Queer Lake is queer only in that its unusually large peninsula results in a very odd-shaped lake. You'll probably want to trek to the end of the peninsula and go swimming.

DAY 2. From the lean-to (0.0 mi.), travel the 1.0 mi. (1.6 km) back to the Chain Ponds trail junction at the southern end of the lake. Turn right and head west for Windfall Pond. A level, well used trail follows yellow markers through hardwoods. A log walk takes you across a wet area. Still on the level, you walk beside a stream until you reach a junction at 1.3 mi. (2.1 km). An unmarked trail continues straight ahead to the privately owned Hermitage camp. Your trail turns sharply left. Proceeding up a moderately steep grade, you soon descend back to the valley floor. The Hermitage Trail junction is reached at 1.5 mi. (2.4 km). The red-marked Hermitage Trail leads 1.3 mi. (2.1 km) northwest to the West Mountain Trail from Higby Road.

Continue straight ahead on a gradual descent for about 10 minutes, then bear left up a moderate grade. Midway up the grade, the trail swings to the right, following the contour along the ridge. A large meadow can be seen down below to your right through the trees. Walking is easy and rate of travel is rapid from this point onward. Soon Windfall Pond is seen below you to the left, sitting in a sheltered basin. Circling down to it, you reach an informal campsite beside its outlet at 2.7 mi. (4.4 km). The Chain Pond Loop junction is just across the outlet.

From here, you return the 1.1 mi. (1.8 km) to Big Moose Road, previously described on Day 1. This is reached at 3.8 mi. (4.2 km).

Chub Pond—Mays Pond Loop

Difficulty: Easy, Day 1; moderately difficult, Day 2
Round Trip Distance: 10.1 mi. (16.4 km)
Time Necessary: 2 days
Map: ADK West-Central Region map; Eagle Bay 7.5'; Eagle Bay metric; Big Moose 15'

On this outing the backpacker visits several pristine bodies of wilderness water. No lean-tos are available at the recommended camping spots, so a tent is essential. Small sections of private land will be crossed on the way to state land; the hiker is urged to treat them with respect as continued access is dependent upon how each person uses this privilege.

Day 1 has extremely flat walking. Should you simply return by the same route, it will be an easy trip; however, you will miss seeing some beautiful forest and several large ponds. Day 2 requires crossing a divide twice. A few spots are slow going with a full backpack, but there are suitable stopping points for lunch, swimming, or fishing, and a relaxed pace should smooth out the trip. Bear in mind that the journey through the woods should be more important than the destination.

Access to the trailhead is off Higby Road at Big Moose Lake. Higby Road is 3.9 mi. (6.3 km) from Eagle Bay on the Big Moose Road. It may not have a sign, but it is the first blacktop road you come to on the right and is a prominent intersection. Travel 1.3 mi. (2.1 km) along Higby Road to a barrier on right which is at privately owned Judson Road. This is the trailhead. Park on the shoulder of Higby Road.

DAY 1. From the trailhead (0.0 mi.), follow the blue-marked trail 100 yds. (92 m) to the privately owned Judson Road. Turn right and walk along this gravel road 0.2 mi. (0.3 km). Just before the road crosses Constable Creek by bridge, an old logging road branches right at a curve in the road.

Turn onto this logging road and continue following blue trail markers. Your course will weave along Constable Creek all the way to its source at Constable Pond. Enroute, the stream has sections that pass through lush vleis and attractive beaver ponds.

A barrier at 0.3 mi. (0.5 km) signifies that state land has been reached. The rocky logging road intersects the red-marked Hermitage Trail to Queer Lake at 0.5 mi. (0.8 km). Soon after, you leave the road you have been walking on and cross Constable Creek on an interesting rustic bridge.

Reentering private land, the trail is now a most pleasant path beside Constable Creek. Spruce and balsam fir give off fragrant scents. The trail merges with a logging road entering from the left at 0.9 mi. (1.5 km). Note this junction, since it is easy to miss on the return trip. The grassy road curves back to Constable Creek and crosses it on a large bridge. There is an interesting wooden fish barrier dam across the creek at this point. Its purpose is to keep undesirable, aggressive fish from migrating upstream, where they could affect trout populations in the upper watershed.

Across the bridge, the blue-marked trail immediately leaves the road and forks left into the woods. Constable Creek passes through a vlei, beaver dam, and beaver pond, all passed on their right. The Mays Pond trail comes in from the right at I.3 mi. (2.I km).

Continuing straight ahead, the trail becomes rocky and footing must be more carefully watched. About 15 minutes later Constable Pond, more a fair-sized lake than a pond, is seen ahead through the trees. Proceeding along the south side of the pond, you find small changes in elevation for the next 10 minutes. A small path leads to the shore at one point, just before the Chub Pond junction is reached at 2.5 mi. (4.1 km). Should you continue straight ahead past the junction another 70 yds. (64 m), you will reach the only campsite to be found on this pond. Pigeon Lake and West Mountain are farther along the blue-marked trail.

The trail to Chub Pond (Lake) follows the yellow-marked trail to the right at the junction. (USGS maps in 1903, and other maps until at least 1941 as well as the current "DEC Trails in the Old Forge-Big Moose Region" pamphlet, all call it Chub Pond. The 1954 USGS map and some current DEC trail signs call it Chub Lake. Hikers traditionally call it Chub Pond.)

Rolling terrain gradually gains elevation to a junction at 2.9 mi. (4.7 km). The trail right continues to Queer Lake. Turn left and follow the trail over a knoll and down to the excellent informal campsite on the edge of Chub Pond at 3.1 mi. (5.0 km).

Set in spruces, a more picturesque setting would be hard to conjure up. A well-built fireplace is safely positioned out on the rock shelf that overlooks the pond. This rock gradually slopes into the water, making an ideal entry place for swimming. Across the very large pond a beaver house is seen near the distant shore. Loons cruise silently, keeping a sharp eye on you as they fish.

DAY 2. A midmorning start will get you to Queer Lake in time for a swim before lunch. Leaving the campsite (0.0 mi.), return to the trail junction at 0.2 mi. (0.3 km) and head south for Queer Lake. At 0.4 mi. (0.6 km), cross a wide inlet of Chub Pond on an elevated log bridge. A vlei is to the right, and the pond stretches out on your left. Proceed up a moderate grade, rounding the south side of the pond. A good view of the water is seen at 0.6 mi. (1.0 km). The trail descends briefly to a stream crossing and then starts a climb up a moderate grade of some length.

The divide between the Raquette River and the Moose–Black River watersheds is reached at I.I mi. (1.8 km). From this height of land a long gradual loss of elevation is found as you continue to Queer Lake. Occasional rises occur, but the general course is a relaxing, easy walk through a marvelous hardwood forest.

The Queer Lake lean-to trail junction is reached at 2.5 mi. (4.1 km). Turn left and drop down to lake level. This red-marked trail extends 0.3 mi. (0.5 km) out to the neck of a long peninsula where the lean-to is located. Several opportunities are possible here. It is an ideal place for a swim and lunch break. There is also an interesting walk out to the end of the peninsula, where there are other swimming and camping sites.

Following this rest break, return the 0.3 mi. (0.5 km) to the last trail junction, which now becomes the 3.1 mi. (5.0 km) point of the hike. This time, bear left at the junction and follow yellow markers on generally level terrain to the Mays Pond junction. This is reached at 3.4 mi. (5.5 km).

Turn right at this junction. Again following yellow trail markers, begin a moderate ascent up a ridge. The early going requires close attention to trail markers. Brushy vegetation and a few blowdowns may cause some concern about the trail ahead. In a few minutes, however, the route improves. It is the least used of the trails you will encounter, and as the hiker use decreases, the wilderness quality of the forest and enjoyment of the hike increases.

The rough climb levels at 3.7 mi. (6.0 km), when you again cross the Raquette River and the Moose-Black River watersheds divide. This is followed by a long, enjoyable, gradual descent to Mays Pond, during which over 300 ft. (92 m) of elevation is lost. This more than compensates for the climb to the height of land you have just completed.

At 4.1 mi. (6.6 km), Mays Pond comes into view. A rocky inlet of the pond is crossed. This large pond is surrounded in this section by thick spruce growth. A few spur trails lead to the water's edge, where one can fish or swim. No good camping sites are readily evident along the trail, but some could be made inland a way and up from the shore.

The trail parallels the eastern shore through sweet-smelling spruces before swinging upslope again at 4.3 mi. (7.0 km). This time the climb is shorter, and only a little over 100 ft. (31 m) in elevation is gained before height of land is reached. The trail veers to the left. A gradual drop takes you to the West Mountain trail junction at 5.7 mi. (9.2 km).

Here, you retrace your previously traveled route to the trailhead by turning left and heading for Higby Road. This last level stretch is enjoyable after the climbing and is quite easy. The trailhead is reached at 7.0 mi. (11.3 km).

To Cold River Trail
& Shattuck Clearing

Moose Pond

Shaw Pond

Black Pond

Wolf Pond Mt.

Moose Mt.

Ward Pond

Newcomb Lake

Baldwin Mt.

Lower Duck Hole

Newcomb River

Rich Lake

Lake Harris

P

28N

To Long Lake

Newcomb Village

Hudson River

N

0   ½   1
Scale in miles

To North Hudson & I-87

Santanoni Preserve

9. The Santanoni Preserve

Santanoni Preserve Options
Difficulty: Easy
Maps: Newcomb 15' Series, Santanoni 15' Series, Newcomb metric

The Santanoni Preserve is a good place for beginners to sharpen their backpacking skills. The terrain varies from level to gradual grades for the most part. Most trails follow dirt roads or old logging trails that are slowly closing in as trees encroach.

The story of how the Santanoni Preserve came into state ownership is heartwarming. It reveals what private citizens with high personal ideals for the public good can do when they are well organized. When the preserve was put up for sale, there was great concern that whoever purchased it might greatly alter its use and character.

In 1971 the Adirondack Conservancy (a subdivision of the Nature Conservancy) decided to gain control of the property so that it could be resold to the state when financial arrangements could be made. The selling party agreed to sell the property for a little over half its appraised value with the understanding that it would remain in its natural state. A grant from the United States Bureau of Outdoor Recreation was applied for and received. The remaining funds for purchase were raised by the Nature Conservancy and Trout Unlimited. Hence, the land was saved and turned over to the state in 1972. It is now part of the Forest Preserve, where it will be forever wild.

Access to the Santanoni Preserve is off Rte. 28N, at the western edge of the village of Newcomb. Turn north at the road junction when you see the Santanoni Preserve sign. Soon after crossing the bridge, you arrive at the handsome stone caretaker's building with a parking area up the grade at right. There are privies up the road from the parking area and a trail register at the trailhead barrier fence.

The preserve is used for hiking, fishing, horseback riding, and skiing. Its trails are extremely well suited to cross-country skiing. Hunting is allowed in season. Fishing is permitted, but without fish bait, from ice out until September 30th.

No special permits for day use or camping are required. The same DEC regulations now apply here as for other state-owned land in the Forest Preserve. Designated campsites are located along the road to Newcomb Lake and at Moose Pond. Trails lead around both sides of Newcomb Lake and there are two lean-tos at the west end of the lake. From the gate, it is 4.7 mi. (7.6 km) to Newcomb Lake. Boating is permitted, but no motors are allowed. Moose Pond is 6.0 mi. (9.7 km) from the gate. The connected series of buildings at Newcomb Lake is not open to the public. (The Town of

Newcomb is currently trying to arrange tours for the public in summer months. When or if this will occur is not known at this time [1995].)

No specific trips are described here because neither the distances involved nor the hiking routes used are difficult to travel. The Moose Pond Horse Trail continues to the Cold River Horse Trail and Shattuck Clearing. It is often used for access into the Cold River country.

Cross-country skiing is excellent throughout the preserve. Snowshoers will find many interesting bushwhacks if they are proficient in their compass skills. It is possible to conduct circuit trips through to Harris Lake along old woods roads.

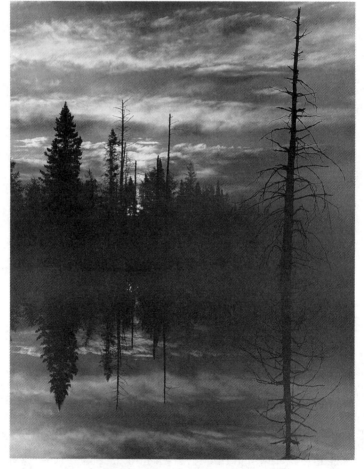

Richard J. Nowicki

Sunrise on Beaver Pond, Moose River Plains

10. High Peaks Wilderness Area

The most physically challenging backpacking in the Adirondack Park is found in the High Peaks Wilderness Area. Before entering this region, it is wise to remember that optimal pleasure comes when the individual's physical stamina matches the toughness of the terrain. Only well conditioned backpackers should take overnight gear into this country. For the many exhausted neophytes who chose the wrong territory to begin their outdoor experiences, blisters, frustration, and often serious injury have been their only rewards.

It is recommended that the novice to the High Peaks first take a few day hikes to determine the size of the challenge. Carry a light day pack over some of these trails. Then decide how far and over what elevation changes you can haul 30 to 40 pounds and still call it fun. This is truly magnificent country, but meet it on terms that are in your favor.

There are three primary points of entry to the High Peaks Wilderness Area. Tahawus is off Rte. 28N in the south near Newcomb. The Garden is a parking area for trails leading through the Johns Brook Valley near the village of Keene Valley on Route 73. The third entry point is outside of Lake Placid, off Rte. 73 at Heart Lake. All three locations are marked with large DEC signposts at the turn-off points from the main highway. The Garden and Heart Lake access areas are frequently crowded on weekends. Midweek hikers will find far fewer parking problems.

The two trips described here give backpackers a good introduction to the region. If this country proves to suit your fancy, you'll soon purchase a copy of Guide to Adirondack Trails: High Peaks Region. This ADK publication has trail descriptions of the whole High Peaks region and includes the ADK topographical trail map, "Trails of the Adirondack High Peak Region".

It is easy to assume that all manner of help will be available should an emergency occur. After all, at any given time in the summer months there may be hundreds of hikers spread throughout this region. There is, however, a vast difference between simply having the presence of numerous individuals and of having qualified, knowledgeable help. Trained personnel for evacuation operations take time to organize. Serious injury may require a dozen or more rescuers or even a helicopter assist from nearby Fort Drum. It is not unusual for 12 to 24 hours of time to be required to mobilize help, depending on the weather and the season. Do not take unnecessary chances here. Carry a good first-aid kit and know how to use it.

The last general concern you should have is how to deal with bears. Bears learn to frequent campsites where food is available. Follow the normal procedures discussed elsewhere in this guide to reduce your problems. Do not get careless in this regard. In this high-density hiking area, you will encounter bears sooner or later.

There are over 170 mi. (275 km) of foot trails in the High Peaks Wilderness Area. The trails described here vary considerably in terrain, difficulty, and locale. This is intended, so that you may appreciate the enormous potential this region offers to backpackers.

Unless you are in excellent physical condition, you are not advised to try scaling 4000 ft. (1223 m) peaks with a full pack. Carry plenty of water. Set a relaxed pace and rest before you become exhausted. A good rule of thumb is to take a 15-minute break every 45 minutes. The average rate of travel in the mountains with full pack is 1.5 mi. (2.4 km) per hour, adding one half hour for each 1000 ft. (306 m) of elevation gained.

Both hikes presented here are challenging when carrying a full pack, but the scenery awaiting the backpacker is magnificent.

Duck Hole via Henderson Lake

Round trip distance: 13.6 mi. (22.0 km)
Time Necessary: 2 days
Map: Mount Marcy Metric or ADK's "Trails of the Adirondack
High Peak Region"

Duck Hole is thought by many to be the most beautiful body of water in the Adirondack backcountry. Deep blue, it is a jewel surrounded by conifers that climb ever higher up the trailless peaks that protect it. Its history, like most Adirondackana, began in the lumber camps of the late 1800s. Loggers cut their way into this region from Long Lake, 16 miles to the southwest. Camps sprang up at Pine Brook, Shattuck Clearing, and Mountain Pond. The lumberjacks pushed up the Cold River Valley. A dam was built at Duck Hole to back up water for spring log runs.

These environs have been a favorite of backpackers since the late 1800s, when Mitchell Sabattis guided for "hunting sports" of the time. In 1977, when the DEC burned its own ranger station here and another at Shattuck Clearing, the attention of just about everyone was riveted on this symbol of wilderness in the Adirondacks. But in wilderness, man is a visitor. Permanent manmade structures conform neither to the concept nor the legal definition of Wilderness. The station was removed to make the area more truly wild and less civilized. There are few who haven't voiced an opinion on this issue. Some hikers miss the greater security a manned station provided, but few would argue the fact that a sense of true wilderness now exists here.

Hikers to this place must be self-sufficient. It is a special place. Be responsible for maintaining and protecting its integrity.

Trail access is off Route 28N, a few miles east of Newcomb. Turn north at the large DEC Tahawus sign. Bear left at the fork that appears 1.6 mi. (2.6 km) from Rte 28N. (The right fork takes you about 20 mi. [32.4 km] over

High Peaks Wilderness Area: Duck Hole via Henderson Lake

Blue Ridge Rd. to the Northway [I-87].) At 7.3 mi. (11.8 km), turn left from the main road just before the road crosses a small bridge over the tiny Hudson River. There is a sign for "Marcy and the High Peaks." This narrow road dead-ends in a large Upper Works parking area after 3.5 mi. (5.7 km) of a winding drive.

The route consists of a portion of the Indian Pass Trail, the Henderson Lake–Preston Pond Trail and a final leg to Duck Hole via the Northville–Placid Trail. Trail conditions vary greatly along the way. Allow plenty of time.

DAY 1. Leaving the Upper Works parking area, head north past the information kiosk and trail register. Continue straight ahead. At 0.1 mi. (0.2 km), where the former trail forks to the right, go straight ahead instead on the loose stone roadway over the outlet of Henderson Lake. Bear right, past the bridge and at 0.2 mi. (0.3 km) continue straight ahead from a junction. (The Calamity Brook Trail branches right here and heads toward the Flowed Lands.)

Recent logging on this private land has made the next mile of travel temporarily unattractive. A few yellow trail markers may be found to guide you, but they are not really needed.

The Henderson Lake–Preston Ponds Trail junction is at 1.5 mi. (2.4 km). The trail turns abruptly left and heads west with red trail markers. It soon crosses Indian Pass Brook on a rather unique large log bridge.

Turning left, a nearly level route is easily traveled via an excellent bridge network. A beaver flow is crossed at 1.8 mi. (2.9 km) and then a minor ascent occurs. No camping is permitted on this private land.

A sharp turn right occurs at 2.1 mi. (3.4 km), and your trail swings to the right. (The trail left leads to a private dock on Henderson Lake.) A brook is crossed several times on bridges before a moderate grade gains elevation at 2.9 mi. (4.7 km). The climb levels at 3.3 mi. (5.3 km) and after a slight descent is again mostly level for awhile. Another slight descent takes you into a wet area and a junction at 3.5 mi. (5.7 km). The trail makes a sharp right turn. (The trail straight ahead leads to a private dock on the Preston Ponds.)

The route to Duck Hole gradually gains elevation as it parallels the outlet of Hunter Pond, which it crosses at 3.9 mi. (6.3 km). After edging around the pond, a short steep pitch leads to the top of a pass at 4.3 mi. (7.0 km). The trail then drops down around a beaver pond to join an old lumber road, which takes you through a wet eroded section. Remnants of the old Piche's lumber camp are found at 4.7 mi. (7.6 km).

Crossing to the right side of the brook, the trail continues to descend with increasing steepness. Lower Preston Pond becomes visible through the trees.

A small swamp is crossed before state land is entered at 5.7 mi. (9.2 km). Another minor descent, followed by an ascent and second descent, finally brings you to the northeast shore of Duck Hole at 5.9 mi. (9.6 km).

Swinging north, a series of ups and downs is negotiated before the left bank of Roaring Brook is reached at 6.4 mi. (10.4 km). The bridge across Roaring Brook periodically washes out and is then replaced. In times of low water, rock hopping Roaring Brook is not a major problem, but during high water periods you will find the stream was well named. Caution must be taken at these times.

Across Roaring Brook is a junction with the Northville–Placid Trail. Turn left. The trail from here to Duck Hole will seem quite easy after what you have just hiked. The route leads downstream and reaches the Ward Brook Fire Road within sight of Duck Hole at 6.8 mi. (11.0 km). Turn left and drop down the short grade to the clearing at Duck Hole. A lean-to and trail register are at the right. Beyond the lean-to is a bridge over the Cold River dam and the beginning of the semi-bushwhack Bradley Pond Trail. (This difficult and mostly unmaintained trail leads 8.2 mi. [13.2 km] to the Tahawus Road) A new second lean-to is located on the north side of the clearing along the tree line.

DAY 2. It might be interesting to walk a short way along the Bradley Pond Trail before returning to Duck Hole, but this route is not recommended unless the hiker is used to bushwhacking. There are some open sections, but about half of the distance to Bradley Pond lean-to is poorly marked and is heavily grown in, due to lack of trail maintenance.

Indian Pass–Lake Colden Loop

Difficulty: Varies from moderate to difficult
Round Trip Distance: 20.6 mi. (33.3 km)
Time Necessary: 3 days with variations
Map: ADK High Peaks Region map; North Elba 7.5', Street Mountain 7.5', Mount Adams 7.5', and Mount Marcy 7.5'; Keene Valley, Ampersand Lake, Santononi Peak and Mount Marcy metrics; Mount Marcy 15', and Santanoni 15'

The Indian Pass–Lake Colden Loop offers an infinite variety of possibilities for shortening, lengthening, toughening, or easing a backpacking trip. The described route is presented because it lends itself to many of these variations. The final trip itinerary is left to the whims and desires of the backpacker.

One of the more interesting, but not immediately obvious, variations is the so-called "toothbrush hike." You begin at Tahawus and hike through Indian Pass to the Adirondack Mountain Club's Adirondak Loj, where you spend the night. (The Loj came by its unusual spelling due to the phonetic spelling preference of Melville Dewey. This system did not survive as long as did his Dewey Decimal System for cataloging library materials.) The next day you return to Tahawus via Lake Colden. With lunch and bathing suit in your day pack, the only overnight gear you need is a toothbrush. Be sure to make prior reservations at the Loj.

If you have heard of the High Peaks, you've probably heard of Lake

High Peaks Wilderness Area: Indian Pass–Lake Colden Loop

Colden. Indian Pass isn't as well known, but it should be. The wild, un-tamed boulder-ridden gorge, mid-August snow-laden caves, and the stupen-dous thousand-foot precipice of Wallface Mountain are natural wonders found nowhere else in the Adirondacks.

Trailhead access is from the Adirondak Loj at Heart Lake. A large DEC sign, "Trail to the High Peaks," 4.0 mi. (6.5 km) southeast of Lake Placid off Route 73, marks the turn-off for Heart Lake. As you travel the open section of the road, you can see the sharp profile of Wallface Mountain at Indian Pass to your right front. To its left is Algonquin, with Avalanche Pass and Lake Colden to its left. Heart Lake, elevation 2178 ft. (666 m), is 4.8 mi. (7.8 km) along Adirondak Loj Road.

At Heart Lake, meals and lodging can be had at the Loj. A large parking area is available for a daily use fee, and the public has free use of the High Peaks Information Center, which provides a source of trail supplies and emergency help when needed.

DAY 1. From the entrance of the public parking area, hike 0.1 mi. (0.2 km) back along Adirondak Loj Road to the trail sign on the left for Indian Pass. Proceed westward from this junction (0.0 mi.), following red DEC trail mark-ers. You soon reach a T-junction, where you make a right turn. Crossing a bridge, you see the trail up Mount Jo to the right. Walk straight ahead around the north shore of Heart Lake. At the end of this pretty little lake, at 0.4 mi. (0.6 km), the old Nye Ski Trail is passed. It was used for the 1932 Olympics.

Continuing to the southwest on the broader red-marked trail, you begin to climb as the Forest Preserve boundary is passed. The excellent trail is generally quite easy. At 2.1 mi. (3.4 km) a side trail leads 0.3 mi. (0.5 km) to the right to Rocky Falls Lean-to.

Climbing now becomes moderate and a second turn-off to Rocky Falls is passed at 2.3 mi. (3.7 km). After crossing several creeks, Scotts Clearing Lean-to is reached at 3.8 mi. (6.1 km). Turning right, you cross the brook in front of the lean-to.

You soon reach a junction where the foundation of the original Scotts Clearing Lean-to is still evident. Bear right and walk over to Scotts Clearing, a few more yards ahead of you. An enormous old stone dam across Indian Pass Brook and a large camping area are located here. This is a very attrac-tive spot and good place to take a long rest break before beginning the hard climb ahead. If an extra day is available or if you had a late start, this is a good tenting area in which to spend the night. The trail to Scott and Wallface ponds begins at the far end of the dam and makes a good side trip.

From the dam, the original route followed up the east side of Indian Pass Brook. However, beavers know a good thing when they see one. In recent years they've repaired the stone dam, and the result has been a flooded Low Water Route most of some years. If this is the the case, it is suggested that you return to the junction by the old lean-to foundation and take the High Water Route around the obstacle.

From the old lean-to foundation, continue straight ahead. At 4.1 mi. (6.6 km) another trail from the clearing enters from the right. Some stiff climbing ensues for a short while to a height of land where a moderate descent takes you back toward the brook. Avoid any other side trails that enter. There is a splendid view of the old dam through the trees. After reaching a second height of land, you make a rather steep descent to rejoin the Lower Water Route at 4.5 mi. (7.3 km).

The trail then parallels Indian Pass Brook, crossing both tributaries and brook frequently. At 4.9 mi. (8.1 km) the crossover Algonquin Pass Trail between Iroquois Peak and Mount Marshall enters from the left. (This 3.3 mi. [5.4 km] trail terminates near the Lake Colden ranger station. It is very steep, ascending 1260 ft. [385 m] enroute.) From this point, climbing becomes very rugged. Take your time and rest when necessary.

After two more stream crossings, the trail narrows and steepens. Climbing over and around large boulders, you encounter some 400 ft. (122 m) of vertical ascent in the next 0.4 mi. (0.6 km). The trail finally levels just before reaching height of land. Look for ice caverns in the deepest parts of this section. Refreshing drafts of cool air stream out of them even in August.

At 5.5 mi. (8.9 km), a DEC sign indicates the high point of the pass has been reached. Elevation is 2834 ft. (867 m). This is some 656 ft. (201 m) above Heart Lake.

By this time, most hikers will have begun to be somewhat awe inspired. Even the blockhouse-size boulders, ice caverns, and rugged trail don't prepare you for the marvelous cliffs of Wallface Mountain. It's no surprise that in 1840 Ebenezer Emmons stated in his first Natural History Survey of the Adirondacks that he was more impressed by "the view of the simple naked rock of Adirondack Pass (Indian Pass)" than he had been previously by Niagara Falls. This imposing rock wall increasingly rivets your attention as you proceed and as its relative position changes with respect to the trail.

The trail dips a little, rises, and finally begins a gradual descent past unbelievably gigantic boulders. At 6.0 mi. (9.1 km) you reach Summit Rock. A very short side trail to the right takes you over a rocky incline to a broad sloping ledge. Here an extremely fine view presents itself down the valley toward Henderson Lake, while up the valley on the left is Wallface Mountain and its distant cliffs. In the far distance down the valley Santanoni Peak, Panther Peak, and Henderson Mountain reach into the sky. Take a long rest break here and enjoy the vista.

From Summit Rock the trail descends steeply. In the next 0.5 mi. (0.8 km) you will lose 450 ft. (138 m) elevation. Ladders occasionally appear and are used to get by the immense boulders found here. At 6.5 mi. (10.5 km) you cross Indian Pass Brook. (This Indian Pass Brook flows into Lake Henderson; do not confuse it with the Indian Pass Brook on the opposite side of the pass, which flows into the West Branch of the Ausable River.)

The trail levels somewhat. It recrosses Indian Pass Brook, various tributaries, and the outlet of Wallface Pond. Finally, at 7.7 mi. (12.5 km), Wallface Lean-to is reached on the right bank of Indian Pass Brook.

It is recommended that you camp here for the night. Henderson Lean-to is another 1.0 mi. (1.6 km) farther down the trail.

DAY 2. From Wallface Lean-to, continue down the pass. At 0.5 mi. (0.8 km.) you will negotiate a short, very steep downgrade. At the bottom, remnants of the old trail are seen straight ahead, but a sign indicates a bridge will be found by taking a fork to the left. You soon cross the bridge over Indian Pass Brook and, after a few more turns in the trail, reach a junction with the Indian Pass-Calamity Brook Passover Trail. (Turning left and using this trail to reach the Calamity Brook Trail saves about a mile of hiking but requires one to climb over a ridge and circumvent a beaver swamp. This is not recommended.)

Bear right from the junction and stay on the red-marked trail you have been traveling. Henderson Lean-to is close to Indian Pass Brook at I .0 mi. (1.6 km). The hiking trail passes by the left side of the lean-to and soon turns right. The trail now enters private land.

Duck Hole trail junction is reached on the right at 1.1 mi. (1.8 km). Follow the trail straight ahead, which now has yellow trail markers. Recent lumbering has temporarily destroyed the forest atmosphere for over a mile. The route gradually ascends and descends. At the top of the next incline, at 2.2 mi. (3.6 km), is the Calamity Brook junction. Upper Works is straight ahead.

Turn left at this junction and follow red markers northeast on the Calamity Brook trail. A swaying suspension bridge crosses Calamity Brook at 3.1 mi. (5.0 km). At times of low water, it might be easier to simply rock-hop the stream. The brook is recrossed on a solid log bridge at 3.7 mi. (6.0 km) and the junction with the cross-over trail from Indian Pass is found just beyond the bridge. There has been recent logging in this area (1995).

Following a blue-marked trail, turn right and head upstream beside the brook. A secondary stream is crossed before the trail joins an abandoned tote road. In a series of moderate grades and intervening level sections the trail begins a lengthy ascent. A short drop in elevation then brings you down steeply to a suspension bridge at 4.8 mi. (7.8 km).

Climbing again commences to height of land, where at 5.7 mi. (9.2 km) you head downward a short way to Calamity Pond. At the far end of the pond, a short trail leads to the pond's edge, where an interesting monument is located. It was placed on this spot by the children of David Henderson who, while on a hunting trip in 1845, was accidently shot and killed. Hence, the name Calamity Pond.

The trail continues with few ups and downs to the shore of the Flowed Lands at 6.2 mi. (10.0 km). Far down the flow, Mount Colden rises in the distance, its naked shoulders profiled against the open sky. The two Calamity Brook lean-tos are found here and Flowed Lands Lean-to is a few minutes walk down the red-marked trail to the right. Two more lean-tos are farther along the Flowed Lands before the dam.

Flowed Lands was drained in late summer 1980 so that the deteriorating dam at its outlet could be inspected. When it is filled with water, the view of Mount Colden from its southern end is one of the most beautiful in the mountains. If Flowed Lands is left in its drained state to become a meadow, the view will also be beautiful for many years until trees grow in and close it off. Whether to remove or repair the dam is but one of the difficult decisions that must be made concerning the High Peaks Wilderness Area in the next few years. The dam at Lake Colden was replaced in the summer of 1980 after washing out the previous spring during melt-off.

The Lake Colden and Marcy Dam areas are heavily used in the summer months. Enforced restrictions are placed upon the number of campers permitted to camp overnight in these two areas. While the hiker usually has no difficulty finding an open lean-to or a designated tenting site, it is not advisable to bypass an available site when the hour is late in the afternoon. Don't try to squeeze out that extra mile or two or you may be walking half the night trying to find another open spot.

For purposes of this trail description, Day 2 will continue to the ranger's cabin at Lake Colden. It is assumed, however, that campers will select an overnight camping spot at some point between Flowed Lands and the cabin.

From the Flowed Lands shore, turn left and cross the bridge over Calamity Brook's outlet into the Flowed Lands. Several informal campsites are in this immediate area just over the bridge. An easy hiking route follows red trail markers 0.4 mi. (0.6 km) to where it climbs over a low ridge.

A rocky section takes you down again to lake level. Herbert Brook is crossed at 7.0 mi. (11.3 km). (Herbert Brook is the usual ascent route up trailless Mount Marshall.)

Another low ridge and then a swampy area are crossed. At 7.3 mi. (11.8 km.), the rocky edge above the crib dam at Lake Colden outlet is reached. This is a major trail junction on the route up Mount Marcy. There are more lean-tos across the dam. These are reached by descending the ladder, crossing the outlet dam, and then crossing the crib dam over the Opalescent to another trail junction. The trail to the right of this junction leads to three lean-tos on the Opalescent River.

Continuing along the west side of Lake Colden, you now follow blue trail markers. West (Cedar Point) Lean-to is reached at 7.4 mi. (12.0 km). Beaver Point Lean-to is 53 yds. (48 m) further on. Side trails lead to both lean-tos. Magnificent views of Mount Colden appear as you climb over the small Beaver Point promontory. Designated tent sites are found in the area ahead. Tenting may be done only at such sites.

The way is along the lake shore. A small bog is crossed just before the trail passes in front of the ranger's cabin at 7.8 mi. (12.6 km). This is the only interior caretaker cabin in the Adirondacks that is staffed throughout the winter months.

DAY 3. From the interior caretaker's cabin (0.0 mi.) the blue-marked trail heads northward towards Marcy Dam. Avoid the crossover trail to Indian Pass via Algonquin Pass that begins near the interior caretaker's cabin. Cold Brook is crossed on a bridge, and the trail junction with the Algonquin Peak trail is reached at 0.2 mi. (0.3 km). Farther along, after crossing the outlet of Avalanche Lake, you reach the junction with the trail from the east side of Lake Colden.

Continue northward towards Avalanche Lake, now following yellow trail markers. The trail heads along the left bank of the outlet, recrossing the outlet at 0.9 mi. (1.5 km) just as Avalanche Lake is approached.

The next 0.5 mi. (0.8 km) is somewhat rough as you scamper over boulders, travel up and down ladders, and perform other nimble-footed tasks while trying not to fall into the lake. On a bridge at 1.1 mi. (1.8 km), you can clearly see the trap dike up Mount Colden across the lake. It offers a challenging route up this formidable peak. Then, at 1.2 mi. (1.9 km), you reach the famous "Hitch-Up-Matilda" bridge. Today, a bridge is firmly bolted to the walls of the pass, but back over a century ago Mr. Fielding kept urging his wife, Matilda, to "Hitch-Up" as Guide Bill Nye struggled to carry her through this then bridgeless section without getting her wet. The upper end of the lake is reached at 1.4 mi. (2.3 km). Soon after, a rock shelter is seen on the right.

As the climb up to the col begins, the walls of the pass close in on you even more. It is a unique experience to thread your way along this narrowing trail. At 2.0 mi. (3.2 km), height of land is reached. Here, the way levels for awhile before beginning the longer descent of over 600 ft. (183 m) to Marcy Dam.

A winter ski trail weaves in and out of this route. Moderate slopes switchback their way downward. A tote road is joined and then the trail parallels the right bank of a tributary of Marcy Brook. Telephone line from the ranger cabin is seen. A wet area is passed on a long log walk.

The junction of the Lake Arnold Crossover trail is reached at 2.5 mi. (4.1 km). The two Avalanche Pass lean-tos are in a large clearing. The trail passes by the lean-tos and crosses Marcy Brook on a wide bridge at the opposite end of the clearing. Turning left, you encounter gradual grades that carry you along at a relaxing pace. In winter the run from the top of Avalanche Pass to Marcy Dam is an outstanding ski route.

Another lean-to is reached at 2.9 mi. (4.7 km), and the trail meets the right bank of Marcy Brook at 3.2 mi. (5.2 km). Leveling off, the trail reaches Marcy Dam at 3.6 mi. (5.8 km). There are seven lean-tos, large group tenting areas, and other designated camping spots here.

Bear left as the blue-marked Van Hoevenberg trail to Marcy merges with your trail from the right. The holding dam for logs from earlier times is reached at 3.8 mi. (6.2 km). A trail register and ranger's cabin are located beside the dam. A water spigot is found at the base of the dam on the outflow side. Standing on the walk across the dam on an early autumn morning, when frost covers the mountain tops and the colored reflections of thousands of trees are seen in the water, is an incomparable experience.

At the far end of the dam, the Van Hoevenberg trail turns right, climbing a rise as it begins the remaining 2.2 mi. (3.6 km) to Adirondak Loj.

You drop down the rise to the rocky edge of Marcy Brook at 4.1 mi. (6.6 km). The trail then meanders gently over several knolls. A bridge with a railing is crossed at 4.5 mi. (7.3 km) and a trail junction is reached at 5.0 mi. (8.1 km). The route to the left heads up Algonquin Peak. Straight ahead is the old route to the Loj.

Turn right and follow the route above the right bank of MacIntyre Brook. A moderate grade takes you down to a crossing of the brook at 5.6 mi. (9.1 km). A second brook is crossed before you briefly join the Hicks Trail (bear right). Follow blue trail signs.

A moderately steep grade takes you to the DEC register and lower parking area at 6.0 mi. (9.7 km). The High Peaks Information Center is directly ahead of you at the opposite end of the clearing.

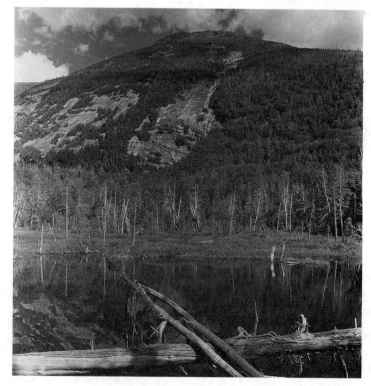

Mount Colden from Lake Colden

Jim Appleyard

11. The Five Ponds Wilderness Area

When the state built Stillwater Reservoir, the flooded lands blocked off access to a huge section of William Seward Webb's lumbering acreage. The state purchased it in compensation, and it thus became part of the Forest Preserve. Today there is a tract of virgin pine, never lumbered or burned, within the Five Ponds Wilderness Area.

Canoeists have long known Cranberry Lake and the Oswegatchie River, but for some reason backpackers have been slow to enter this region in appreciable numbers. It is in many ways unique, which is why folks in the St. Lawrence River country continue to come to their "South Woods" for relaxation and self-renewal.

Hikers who have not been in this region for some time will find several changes in the trail routes. Extreme blowdown during the July 15, 1995, microburst storm resulted in abandonment of the Leary Trail and the reopening of the longer fire truck route to High Falls. It is now called the High Falls Foot Trail.

Prior to the 1995 storm, beaver activity caused the closing of the trail section from Clear Pond to High Falls. The old Plains Trail was moved off the plains and rerouted along the base of Three-Mile Mountain. Such famous destinations as Boiling Springs and Pine Orchards must now be reached by bushwhacking.

Hikers wishing a more comprehensive description of trails in this area will find the ADK *Guide to Adirondack Trails: Northern Region* and the ADK map "Trails of the Northern Region" helpful.

Cowhorn Pond–High Falls Loop

Difficulty: Easy walking, but long
Round Trip Distance: 22.9 mi. (36.6 km)
Time Necessary: 2 long or 3 short days
Maps: ADK Northern Region map; Five Ponds 7.5', Wolf Mountain 7.5', and Newton Falls 7.5'; Cranberry Lake 15'

The trail options on this trip include a short overnighter at Janacks Landing, a side trip up Cat Mountain, and an infinite number of ponds to visit. The circuit could take two weeks if you combined the Five Ponds route with it. The outing described here can be a two-day trip for backpackers who like to push it or a leisurely three-day trip for those who want some fishing or plan to study the "plains" area.

Access to the trailhead is from the village of Wanakena, off Rte. 3 between Star Lake and Cranberry Lake. From Rte. 3, drive 1.0 mi. (1.6 km) south to Wanakena. Bear right at any road forks you come to along the way. A bridge takes you over the Oswegatchie River. From there, travel 0.5 mi. (0.8 km) to a small DEC sign on the right side of the road indicating the Dead Creek Flow Trail. There is a parking area on the right, a few meters beyond the sign and gate.

DAY 1. Begin your hike from the gate (0.0 mi.). Red trail markers guide you along the almost level grassy route. After about 25 minutes of walking, a 0.2 mi. (0.3 km) rerouting of the trail bears left around a beaver pond. A few minutes later you catch your first glimpse of Dead Creek Flow on the left. Your position now is almost at the end of the narrow bay of Cranberry Lake. At 2.0 mi. (3.2 km) the trail narrows. There is a picnic table and fireplace here by the shore of the flow.

A trail bears right, around the end of the flow, and crosses two inlets on log bridges. The route soon moves away from the water and enters hardwoods. At 3.2 mi. (5.2 km) a trail junction is reached. The left-hand turn leads 0.2 mi. (0.3 km) to Janacks Landing, where a lean-to and several good tent sites are found on the shore of Dead Creek Flow.

Hiking straight ahead from the junction, continue to follow red trail markers. The route is flat for about 15 minutes, then you enter a narrow draw and begin a gradual ascent. A spring appears below the left bank of the trail as the steeper grade begins. Near the end of the draw, the grade becomes moderately steep as you climb to height of land.

Just past height of land is Sand Hill Junction at 4.0 mi. (6.5 km). This trail fork could easily be missed if you were not looking for it. The "plains trail" continues down the slope, following blue trail markers.

Turn left at this fork and follow the contour along the side of the ridge. The sound of rushing water is heard as you approach the cascading outlet of Glasby Pond. The trail follows the right bank of the stream. A bridge takes you across the outlet just before you reach the pond at 4.3 mi. (7.0 km) . Glasby Pond, with blueberry bushes surrounding its shores, is most attractive. Its dark waters and the slopes of Cat Mountain across the pond create a primitive setting.

The trail swings by an informal campsite, gains a little elevation, and continues around the south side of the pond. Take time to admire the water as you walk along.

Now heading away from the pond, you slowly gain elevation. At 4.5 mi. (7.3 km) the Cat Mountain trail junction is reached. The trail straight ahead leads 0.6 mi. (1.0 km) up Cat Mountain. This is a very easy climb and is well worth the effort, for the view is excellent.

Turning right from this junction, head southeast and follow yellow trail markers toward Cowhorn Junction. A leaf-covered trail over low rolling grades provides comfortable walking. Before long, you pass some large boulders and notice Cat Mountain Pond to your left at 5.6 mi.

Five Ponds Wilderness Area

(9.1 km). The trail stays well back from the shore of this attractive body of water. Unmarked paths occasionally lead to the shoreline.

At 6.1 mi. (9.9 km) Six Mile Creek, the outlet of Bassout Pond, is crossed on a log bridge. Soon a moderately steep rise takes you up to the top of an esker ridge where Cowhorn Junction is located at 6.5 mi. (10.5 km). Large Cowhorn Pond is seen through the trees far below you to the east.

Turn left at this junction and walk along the top of the ridge, a narrow spine with drop-offs on both sides, to the north. Tall hemlocks and pleasant breezes create an unusually enjoyable section of trail. Another junction is reached at the end of Cowhorn Pond at 6.9 mi. (11.2 km). The trail straight ahead leads 3.8 mi. (6.2 km) to the West Flow of South Bay on Cranberry Lake.

Take the right fork around the shoreline 0.2 mi. (0.3 km) to Cowhorn Pond Lean-to, reached at 7.1 mi. (11.5 km). It sits in a large open clearing, back from the water. There is a sweeping view of the pond from the shelter.

DAY 2. In the first edition of this guidebook, Day 2 covered Cowhorn Junction to Clear Pond, Nick's Pond, Pine Ridge and on to High Falls. (It was in this country that the famous hermit and guide, Fide [Philo] Scott took out the local sports. Scott was the prototype Irving Batcheller used for his 1906 book, Silas Strong, Emperor of the Woods.) In recent years, beaver activity has resulted in DEC's abandonment of this route from Clear Pond to High Falls. The old Plains Trail has been moved to the east edge of the plains. Consequently, on Day 2 High Falls must be reached by returning 3.1 mi. (5.0 km) to Sand Hill Junction. (This is a good time to climb Cat Mountain if you didn't do it on Day 1.)

From Sand Hill Junction, you may simply continue to retrace the Day 1 route back to Wanakena to complete a nice two-day outing. If more time is available, High Falls is a good destination and is described here.

From Sand Hill Junction, turn left and follow blue trail markers southward on the High Falls Loop Trail. The trail loses elevation until it crosses Glasby Creek at the edge of the plains at 3.3 mi. (5.3 km). At 3.5 mi. (5.7 km) it reaches a junction, where the abandoned old Plains Trail bears right. (In time this junction will become less evident.) The newer High Falls Loop Trail swings left from this junction and sidles along the base of Three-mile Mountain.

The route passes over rolling terrain, crossing several creeks without much significant change in elevation. At 5.2 mi. (8.4 km) it passes through a wetlands zone that may give one some concern in times of wet weather. Leaving the wet zone, the trail soon joins the High Falls Foot Trail at 5.6 mi. (9.1 km). Turn left at the junction and follow the wide, red-marked trail first east and then south of the High Falls.

The Oswegatchie River and its most attractive High Falls are reached at 6.2 mi. (9.9 km). There is a lean-to on each side of the river, but the quaint old rustic bridge that used to cross the waterway is no longer present. Several designated camping areas are found along the stream. This is also the destination of many backcountry paddlers, so expect to see people in this area.

Strong hikers may continue on to Wanakena (see Day 3 trail description), but most will spend the night here, exploring a bit and enjoying the region.

DAY 3. To return to Wanakena, retrace yesterday's route 0.6 mi. (1.0 km) to the junction for Sand Hill. Continue past the junction on the High Falls Foot Trail in a generally northwest direction and then, at 1.0 mi. (1.6 km), sharply to the southwest. Glasby Creek is crossed on a bridge at 1.1 mi. (1.8 km). The abandoned Leary Trail junction is passed at 1.6 mi. (2.6 km). Fifty yards further on, the Five Ponds–Sand Lake junction is reached.

Continue straight ahead. The Oswegatchie River is soon in view for a while and an old sand pit is passed before the Cage Lake–Buck Pond junction is reached at 3.3 mi. (5.3 km). (The bridge over the Oswegatchie River collapsed some years ago and this trail is closed [1998]. DEC may reopen this trail in future.)

Sporadic beaver activity may be a factor for the next few miles. High Rock Creek is crossed on an old stone and concrete bridge at 4.9 mi. (7.9 km) and the informal 0.2-mi. (0.3 km) path to the Oswegatchie River may be seen at left at 5.3 mi. (8.6 km). The trail gradually climbs and you may spot an historic marker and cairn marking the 1812 Albany Trail and an even earlier Indian route where it crosses your trail at 6.7 mi. (10.9 km).

After passing height of land, the other end of the abandoned Leary Trail is reached at 7.4 mi. (12.0 km). Still descending, Skate Creek is crossed and the trail levels before a DEC vehicular barrier gate is reached at 9.1 mi. (15.0 km). Another tenth of a mile brings you to the pavement in Wanakena. By turning right and walking another four-tenths mile, you'll reach the parking area for Dead Creek, where you began your hike. Total distance is 6 mi. (15.6 km).

Five Ponds–Sand Lake-Cage Lake Outing

Difficulty: Easy grades, but uneven trail conditions
Round Trip Distance: 35.0 mi. (56.0 km)
Time Necessary: 4 days, if all parts are done
Maps: ADK Northern Region map; Newton Falls 7.5', Five Ponds 7.5',
    and Cranberry Lake 7.5'; Cranberry Lake 15', and
    Oswegatchie 15'

The Five Ponds–Sand Lake–Cage Lake Outing is a true wilderness back-

packing trip. While campers frequently head for the lean-to at Big Shallow, relatively few hikers go on to Sand Lake. Beavers have made the
full circuit to Cage Lake difficult, but for those who want the essence of
true wilderness, this trip can't be beat.

The trip isn't recommended for beginners or those who feel squea-
mish about crossing a bridge that happens to be underwater. In places,
the distance will seem greater than it really is. It isn't a region to rush
through.

Access to the trailhead is from the village of Wanakena. Follow the
same access directions given for the Cowhorn Pond–High Falls Loop to
the bridge over the Oswegatchie River at Wanakena. The High Falls Foot
Trail, where you begin to hike, is 0.1 mi. (0.2 km) past this bridge, on
the right. Continue a short distance past this dirt road to a tennis court.
Just beyond the tennis court is a parking area.

DAY 1. The trail follows red DEC trail markers to a gate 0.1 mi. (0.2
km) along the truck road. The very flat route passes a pond that is on
the left. The slightly raised road has shallow water on both sides in
places before it begins to climb at 0.9 mi. (1.5 km). As you climb the
gradual grade, Skate Creek is visible through the trees below you to the
right.

The route traveled is an old logging railroad bed that gradually climbs
to height of land at 2.0 mi. (3.2 km). After gradual descent, the informal High Rock path going west two–tenths mile to the Oswegatchie
River may be seen at 3.9 mi. (6.3 km). High Rock Creek bridge is crossed
at 4.3 mi. (6.9 km). A low-elevation region, often showing evidence of
beaver activity, is now seen. The Sand Lake–Five Ponds trail junction is
reached at 7.6 mi. (12.3 km). (See page 105, Day 3, for more information about this first section of trail.)

Take this blue-marked trail southwestward toward Five Ponds. After
15 minutes of walking along this route, you'll see a path on the left.
It leads to a very nice informal campsite with a fireplace at the base of a
large boulder.

The main trail curves around a slope to a bridge over the Oswegatchie
River. Another path, near the bridge, also heads to the campsite. Across
the bridge is a second, less desirable, campsite. DEC does not plan on
replacing this bridge if it again washes out or collapses for other reasons. At some time in the future it may be necessary to wade this stream,
which is difficult in high water.

At 8.9 mi. (14.2 km) the trail makes an abrupt left-hand turn at a
junction. Avoid the right side of this junction, which will take you northward to the Oswegatchie River.

A series of log bridges and corduroy takes you through a wet section
in good shape. The outlet of Five Ponds is on the right and is soon

crossed. You briefly climb away from the stream but soon return. The rocky stream is attractive. The route is now squeezed between the water and the steepening wall of the Five Ponds esker at your right. At 10.1 mi. (16.2 km) the trail comes to a shallow ford at the outlet of Big Shallow. Bearing right, along the stream shore, you almost immediately reach the lean-to on this pond. The lean-to stands at the shore with a view across the water. A spring is found a short distance along the path around the right side of the pond. A bushwhack up the side of the esker, past the spring, is a worthwhile venture. Mammoth white pines are found there. You may also want to walk southward along the crest of the esker, where you can drop down to Big Five, or walk northward on the crest, where you can drop down to Little Five. Both of these ponds are on the opposite side of the esker from the lean-to.

Big Shallow Lean-to is a good spot to spend the night. If it's occupied, the trip to the Little Shallow lean-to isn't very far.

DAY 2. From the Big Shallow Lean-to (0.0 mi.), return the short distance to the ford across the outlet of the pond. Cross this creek and climb up the minor grade onto higher ground. About 10 minutes later, the route passes between tiny Washbowl on the left and Little Shallow on the right. Popping over a small ridge brings you to the Little Shallow Lean-to at 0.5 mi. (0.8 km). It sits well up from the water and would be a good choice during black fly season. There is a spring down near the pond.

The trail continues past the lean-to, climbing very gradually. Soon it enters a narrow valley, where a beaver pond is situated. Thereafter, the route levels for a while before resuming the long gradual climb through the still narrow valley. Reaching height of land, the course descends gradually for some distance before the valley finally widens out a bit.

About 10 minutes later, you climb over a small rise and drop down to the Wolf Pond junction at 1.9 mi. (3.1 km). Good fishing, a long sandy beach, and a fine lean-to are good reasons to spend a night at Sand Lake if you have the time.

Taking the left fork, continue to follow blue trail markers. The trail soon turns southward and gradually descends to cross the inlet of Wolf Pond. It then gradually ascends, and Wolf Pond can be seen to the right of the trail at 2.9 mi. (4.7 km). From there it levels for a while, passes a waterfall as it descends again, and then follows a flat trail through excellent woods to Sand Lake. The Sand Lake lean-to is reached at 4.4 mi. (7.1 km). It sits among conifers near the sandy beach of the lake.

A walk around the shoreline to the right will bring you to the esker that separates Sand Lake from Rock Lake. It is interesting that the difference in water sources of these two bodies of water results in greatly varying forms of aquatic life, although they are very close to each other. This is a wonderful place to relax, swim, and enjoy nature.

DAY 3. The day begins with the 2.5 mi. (4.1 km) walk back to the Wolf Pond junction. Take the left-hand fork at Wolf Pond junction. Easy walking lets you quickly cover the 0.5 mi. (0.8 km) to Wolf Pond Lean-to, reached at 3.1 mi. (5.0 km). Wolf Pond is a very sizeable sheet of water. One of the idiosyncrasies of Adirondackana is that a body of water's being called a pond or a lake seems to have little to do with its size. By any normal standards, this is a pretty good-sized lake.

The lean-to sits two or three minutes' walk above Wolf Pond. Large white pines dominate the scene. A side trail behind the lean-to takes you to a spring. It is difficult to get clean water from the pond itself, as it has a rather murky shoreline. A walk down to the shore is most rewarding, however, because the expanse is almost panoramic in scope.

From the lean-to the trail swings right, over a small knoll. It then descends to a wide open valley, through which runs the outlet of Wolf Pond. Currently, crossing this vale has presented no problems. In the recent past, however, beaver activity has completely flooded the area knee-deep with water.

Trail markers exist but are hard to find. The area of possible flooding is only 100 yds. (31 m) long. If the route is not obvious, take a northwest heading on your compass and head out toward the opposite side. Trail markers can be found as high ground is reached.

After making your way over to the far side of the valley, you negotiate a moderate slope on dry ground. The character of the woods begins to change as you reach higher ground. Better soil drainage lets the birches, maples, and beeches grow in abundance.

At about 3.9 mi. (6.3 km) you drop down the steep bank and cross the outlet of Muir Pond. Climbing the opposite bank, you continue through a fine hardwood forest on a comfortable trail.

A gradual loss of elevation brings you to the outlet of Deer Marsh at 4.6 mi. (7.4 km). As you continue northeastward, easy terrain eventually brings you within sight of Cage Lake. Walking near the shoreline for 0.1 mi. (0.2 km), you reach the Cage Lake Lean-to at 5.5 mi. (8.8 km).

The lean-to is a newer prefabricated type, which DEC air-dropped onto the site. It sits up a little way from the lake. A good view of the lake can be had from the clearing.

The hiking trail leads straight ahead down a steep embankment to the lake's outlet stream, where good drinking water is found. The refreshing breeze off the lake and the possibility of a cooling swim make this a good place to spend the night. At the height of the black fly season, on June 22, 1976, Joan Dean left a message on the lean-to ceiling for future hikers to ponder: "There is a rare beauty here that makes it worth the bugs." It is even more enjoyable in August, when there are no bugs.

(Beyond the Cage Lake lean-to, the trail winds generally northward 0.9 mi. (1.5 km) to a junction. From the right fork of the junction, an abandoned trail leads to Cage Lake Springhole on the Oswegatchie River, where a bridge used to permit the hiker to connect up with the High Falls Foot Trail. Since the collapse of the bridge, this trail is no longer maintained. Beaver activity makes its use almost impossible and the hiker is advised to avoid it. The left fork of the junction continues northward 7.5 mi. (12.2 km) to a trailhead on Youngs Rd., 1.9 mi. (3.1 km) south or Rte. 3 at Star Lake village.)

DAY 4. Day 4 is a basic retracing of your footsteps back to the starting point of Day 1. It is a pleasant trip of 15.0 mi. (24.0 km). This could be divided into two days' journey.

Further hiking might take you across the Plains to Janacks Landing for another night out. Then it would be back to Wanakena along Dead Creek Flow. This is a region where many options can be planned for every trail.

Cat Mountain

To Tupper Lake

To
Cranberry
Lake

Bear Mt. Trail

Brandy Brook

Burntbridge
Pond

Burntbridge Outlet

Brandy
Brook
Flow

Hedgehog
Pond

East Creek

Bear
Mt.

Dog Pond
Mt.

Curtis
Pond

Irish
Pond

East Inlet

Willy's
Pond

Dog Pond

Proulx Clearing

0   ½   1
Scale in miles

N

Cranberry Lake Wild Forest

12. The Cranberry Lake Wild Forest Area

Backpackers have long known and hiked the Five Ponds Wilderness Area on the south and west sides of Cranberry Lake. However, few people know that there is now another excellent area for backpacking on the east side of Cranberry Lake, the Cranberry Lake Wild Forest Area.

The Burntbridge Pond Trail is fairly well used by skiers, who ski the snowmobile trail, but it has been used in summer primarily by anglers. With the addition of the Dog Pond Loop, an extensive area now connects the Burntbridge Pond Trail with old logging trails to the south, East Inlet, and Brandy Brook Flow. Such places as Irish Pond, Willys Pond, Dog Pond Mt., Dog Pond, Curtis Pond, and Hedgehog (Clear) Pond are now open to the backpacker.

The Dog Pond Loop via the Burntbridge Pond Trail

Difficulty: Moderate for experienced hikers
Loop Distance: 20.8 mi. (33.7 km)
Time: Three Days
Maps: Cranberry Lake 7.5' and Long Tom Mountain 7.5' or Piercefield metric; Cranberry Lake 15' and Tupper Lake 15'; ADK Northern Region map (limited coverage)

The trip described here is only one of several possible outings. Be aware that while the Burntbridge Pond lean-to is a very nice place to camp, there is not good camping around it. Check the trail registers to find if another group has headed that way ahead of you; if so, it might be wise to take the Dog Pond Loop in a counterclockwise direction, where there will be many more campsites available.

Many hikers will be happy with a few days at Brandy Brook Flow and East Inlet, thereby avoiding the interesting but fairly rigorous section between the east end of the Dog Pond Loop Trail and East Inlet. The trip can be extended by side trips up Dog Pond Mountain or to Dog Pond, if desired.

DAY 1. Access to the Burntbridge Pond Trailhead is off Rte. 3, 2.7 mi. (4.4 km) east of Cranberry Lake village. There is a large DEC signpost, good-sized parking area, and exhibit board.

The trail heads south up a slight grade on a wide trail, following occasional large red snowmobile trail markers. Much of the route used to be a spur of the Grass River Railroad, built by the Emporium Lumber Company. Now it is a grassy roadway and quite pleasant. The route soon levels, though it will eventually gain and then lose about 100 ft. (31 km) elevation before reaching Brandy Brook. At 1.4 mi. (2.3 km), the Bear Mountain Trail comes in from the west. (This side trail leads 2.4 mi. [3.9 km] to the Cranberry Lake

Public Campground and also 3.5 mi. [5.7 km] to the summit of Bear Mountain.) There is a trail register at this junction. A few minutes' travel time beyond this junction, the route passes through an open meadow and then returns to deciduous forest.

The nearly flat course turns sharply right at 2.25 mi. (3.6 km) and sidles around an extensive wetland that drains into Brandy Brook. Then, at 2.8 mi. (4.5 km), a low bridge crosses Brandy Brook. The trail again turns abruptly right, continuing along the brook to 2.85 mi. (4.6 km) where a designated campsite is found at the right side of the trail.

The west junction of the Dog Pond Loop Trail is in a grassy opening at 3.0 mi. (4.9 km). Here the Burntbridge Pond trail turns left, the Dog Pond Loop Trail heads south, and a small unmarked trail leads right about 100 yds. (92 m) to the bank of Brandy Brook Flow, where a canoe landing marks the farthest point up the flow that most paddlers care to travel.

Continuing eastward, the Burntbridge Pond Trail remains a wide path that will gradually gain 250 ft. (76 m) elevation and then lose 150 ft. (45.9 m) of it before reaching Burntbridge Pond. Another designated campsite is found at left, across a small brook and up a small knoll at 4.1 mi. (6.6 km). This is nearly to the high point of elevation gain and is the last designated camping spot before reaching the lean-to. (Since obtaining water at the lean-to is often difficult, you may wish to fill water containers at this brook and take them with you to the lean-to.)

Some elevation loss occurs before the junction with the east end of the Dog Pond Loop, which enters from the south at 5.4 mi. (8.7 km). DEC trail signs are found here.

The Burntbridge Pond Trail continues 0.5 mi. (0.8 km) northeast to an easily missed junction at 5.9 mi. (9.6 km), where the snowmobile trail continues straight ahead, but the trail to the lean-to forks to the right. From here, elevation is steadily lost as the trail swings east and then southeast. A sign on a tree indicates it is 0.3 mi. (0.5 km) to the lean-to, just before a second, unmarked junction is reached. Bear right at this second junction and continue along the track. Another sign indicates Rte. 3 is 6.5 mi. (10.5 km), and a final descent brings you to the lean-to at Burntbridge Pond at 6.6 mi. (10.7 km).

The site of the lean-to is scenic and slightly uphill from the marshy shoreline. There is a small boardwalk to the water source at the pond, but it will be difficult to reach the water, which is shallow. If this water is used, it would be best to filter or treat it before drinking. Further along the shoreline is a better spot for collecting water.

DAY 2. The second day's route is quite different from that of the first day. Day 1 followed established old routes. Day 2 is a true woods path that heads south to connect up with other old established routes. It essentially follows trail markers but requires care in places where the route requires trail work due to blowdowns or new growth. Terrain is more rugged and elevation change is more frequent.

Return 1.2 mi. (1.9 km) to the east end junction of the Dog Pond Loop Trail. From here, turn left and follow blue trail markers of the Dog Pond Loop Trail generally southward. Initially, the trail is quite wide, open and level. At 1.45 mi. (2.3 km) the path reaches a large beaver pond, where a large dam has been built just downstream from where a trail bridge crosses water. In 1993 the bridge stood alone, surrounded by water due to the beaver activity and it was necessary to get around the obstacle by going downstream from the dam.

The trail tends to the southeast and soon begins a gradual to moderate descent to a wooden bridge at 1.95 mi. (3.2 km). Here a wide, shallow brook is negotiated and the route soon swings southwest, continuing descent as it skirts the marshy drainage outlet of Burntbridge Pond. Once this is accomplished, the trail heads due south. At 2.8 mi. (4.5 km) a moderately steep upgrade begins, and the weight of your pack will seem to increase. The slope moderates after 0.2 mi. (0.3 km) but still climbs as the trail passes over the west shoulder of an unnamed bump. It then drops a little before reaching a small brook. This is the source water of East Creek. Just beyond this brook, as the path curves and ascends a small knoll at 3.5 mi. (5.7 km), is another designated campsite, at left.

A steady climb takes you into the col between Bear Mountain and Dog Pond Mountain. The Dog Pond Mountain trail junction is reached at 4.2 mi. (6.8 km) at height of land. (The Dog Pond Mountain trail follows yellow markers 0.3 mi. [0.5 km] up a sometimes slippery trail to an overlook on the side of the mountain. Good views of Center Pond and Center Pond Mountain are found. Summit elevation is 810 ft. [743 m].)

The easy downgrade to Proulx Clearing from the col is welcome after the climbing in the last section of trail. The trail parallels the east side of a marshy tributary of Sucker Brook at 4.9 mi. (7.9 km) until it crosses the Dog Pond outlet, climbs up a small rise, and passes through the open meadow of Proulx Clearing to a DEC signpost at 5.2 mi. (8.4 km). (The path eastward from this signpost leads 0.4 mi. [0.6 km] to Dog Pond. There are several campsites on its shore and a waterfall at its inlet.)

The Dog Pond Loop Trail heads west, dropping down the rise to cross the tributary brook on a small bridge. At 5.8 mi. (9.4 km) the rolling path ends at Irish Pond. (A side trail leads a few hundred yards along the shoreline to a second side trail which leads up a knoll at right to a designated campsite. The shoreline trail continues over a low knoll to the end of the pond, where a natural rock overhang shows evidence of long use as a campsite.)

From Irish Pond, the trail continues west for a while before descending gradually to the southwest. Willys Pond is reached at 6.3 mi. (10.2 km), where its rocky outlet is crossed on a log bridge. This is a particularly impressive body of water with no designated campsites (1994).

The route leads northwest over a knoll from the outlet, climbing gradually over the north shoulder of a small hill before reaching Curtis Pond at 7.0 mi. (11.3 km). The path drops down to the pond outlet and then climbs over a rise, where you can see the full size of the pond. At 7.05 mi. (11.4 km) there is a side trail right to a designated campsite.

The trail reaches the Curtis Pond Trail junction at 7.1 mi. (11.5 km). (This trail comes from the southeast corner of East Inlet on Cranberry Lake.) As you bear right from the junction, rolling terrain takes you northwest until a steady moderate descent begins at 7.5 mi. (12.2 km). An amazing assemblage of glacial erratics, known as Willys Cave, is found at 7.8 mi. (12.6 km). This is not a true cave but rather a group of huge boulders with a very sizeable opening in its center where several people could camp in an emergency.

Descent continues from Willys Cave to a junction just before East Creek at 8.2 mi. (13.3 km). Here a trail right leads 50 yds. (46 m) to a designated campsite along East Creek. Leading in the opposite direction (west) from this junction is a path to a spring, which is not dependable.

A large bridge crosses East Creek. The trail turns left, heading downstream. It eventually curves away from the stream and reaches a junction at 8.35 mi. (13.5 km), where East Inlet can be seen. The unmarked path forking left leads 100 yds. (92 m) to the shore of East Inlet. The Dog Pond Loop Trail curves right and parallels East Inlet, about 100 ft. (31 m) back from the shore. At 8.4 mi. (13.6 km) there is a side path left that leads to Site #14, a very nice designated campsite on the shore of East Inlet. The trail continues along the inlet to 8.7 mi. (14.1 km), where it makes a sharp right inland. The sight of the privy along the trail probably will be the first clue that Campsite #13 has been reached. A path leads several yards back to a very large designated campsite, which gives evidence of much use.

DAY 3. You may wish to spend extra time at East Inlet. The final walk out to Rte. 3 is easy and not far. From Campsite #13 (0.0 mi.) the trail soon reaches a wide inlet, where it is necessary to walk a short way upstream to a crossing place. Then the trail climbs a moderate grade northward. In time, it levels and becomes a very pleasant course, reaching the Hedgehog Pond junction at 0.6 mi. (1.9 km). A path enters from the west, which leads 0.2 mi. (0.3 km) to Hedgehog Bay. It continues 0.2 mi. (0.3 km) east to Hedgehog Pond. (Older maps identify this as Clear Pond.) Long rolling grades continue north until the trail drops down a grade to Brandy Brook Flow. At 1.65 mi. (2.7 km), the trail makes an abrupt right turn. At this point, a designated campsite symbol is seen and a side path leads a short distance to Campsite #10. This attractive site has the remains of a large stone fireplace, the only remaining evidence of what was once the Indian Mountain Club.

The trail climbs a short way from the water. Another designated campsite symbol is seen at 1.9 mi. (3.1 km). Here a very faint path winds its way at an acute angle from the trail to Campsite #9, which occupies the end of a long narrow point on Brandy Brook Flow.

The trail curves northwestward and then has an abrupt turn right at 2.1 mi. (3.4 km). Here the unobservant hiker may miss a designated campsite symbol. A side path leads west, curving around to Campsite #8, the last designated campsite before reaching the Burntbridge Pond Trail junction.

The trail continues generally north from this point. A signed DEC junction is found at 2.3 mi. (3.7 km). (The sharp left turn of the unmarked trail leads to the shore of Brandy Brook Flow and is the snowmobile trail that leads to ice and then Cranberry Lake village in winter.) The Dog Pond Loop Trail continues straight ahead, soon reaching a snowmobile trail sign indicating a curving left turn which you should also follow. A small soggy dip in the trail is crossed, and then the route swings right just before reaching the junction with the Burntbridge Pond Trail at 2.5 mi. (4.1 km). (From here, take the Burntbridge Pond Trail 3.0 mi. [4.9 km] north to the Rte. 3 trailhead. This is the reverse of the first part of the Day 1 trip and is reached at 5.5 mi. [8.9 km].)

Willeys Pond

To Rt. 30 &
Tupper Lake

10A

10A

To Rt. 30
& Long Lake

Little
Tupper
Lake

Private Land

State Land

N

Loon Pond

Bear Pond

10

Sabattis

Charley
Pond

Scale in miles

0   ½   1

Adirondack Railroad

Lake Lila

P

Nehasane

Mt. Frederica

Former
Nehasane
Lodge Site

Beaver River

Nehasane

13. Nehasane

Nehasane *(Ne-haas'in-nee)* is treated here as a separate section. It is anticipated that at least some of this land will eventually become part of the Five Ponds Wilderness Area.

One of the earliest settlers of this part of the Adirondacks was David Smith, a hermit at Smith Lake from 1830-1845. The lake has since been called Lake Lila, after the wife of Dr. Seward Webb. This lake is the largest lake in the Forest Preserve whose perimeter is entirely owned by New York State.

While president of the Wagner Palace Car Company, the manufacturer of Pullman Railroad Cars, Webb started the Adirondack and St. Lawrence Railroad. This was consolidated with the Mohawk and Malone (M & M) Railroad Company, which had a private stop at Nehasane. The railroad eventually closed, but reopened for the 1980 Olympics year. For a short time, a hiker could step off the train at Nehasane and begin hiking. A short section of this railroad still functions near Thendara for summer tourists and plans call for extending the length of usable track in the future. If so, in coming years it may again become possible for the hiker to take a train to Nehasane.

The Nehasane Park Association was created in 1894. The great Nehasane Lodge once housed 25 guests and servants. As an unconforming structure in the Forest Preserve, Nehasane Lodge was burned to the ground in 1984. Webb introduced black-tailed deer and elk to his fenced-in preserve. Gifford Pinchot, the famous early forest management expert, wrote his book *The Adirondack Spruce* while employed at Nehasane. It was the first American publication to explain how European forest management systems could be applied in the United States.

Nehasane

Difficulty: Easy canoeing, hard backpacking
Time Needed: Variable
Maps: Big Moose 15' Series and Five Ponds 15' Series or
Little Tupper Lake metric and Wolf Mountain 7.5' Series.

Access to Nehasane is off Rte. 30 between Long Lake and Tupper Lake. Whichever direction you are coming from, turn west on either of the two roads (0.0 mi.) having signs indicating the direction to Sabattis. They merge after 3.I mi. (5.0 km) at Little Tupper Lake, continuing as County Road 10 down the north side of the lake for Sabattis. The headquarters for Whitney Park is passed at 4.4 mi. (7.1 km). Be careful not to miss the turnoff for Nehasane Park as you come down a dip in the road at 8.3 mi. (13.4 km).

Turn left onto the dirt road and proceed another 5.6 mi. (9.1 km) to a DEC parking area near Lake Lila. A gate at the opposite end of the parking area prevents further vehicular traffic. No trailers for camping or boats are permitted here. No hunting on surrounding private lands is permitted, whether or not the land has been posted.

Maps of Lake Lila are available at the DEC trail register in the parking area, and a park ranger is generally on duty in the area in the summer. A trail from the parking area leads 0.3 mi. (0.5 km) down a slight grade to the sandy beach on Lake Lila. Here canoes and other nonmotorized watercraft can be put into the water. Only cartop-carried craft are allowed.

Camping is permitted at 17 areas around the shoreline and on four islands. Each site is indicated by yellow designated campsite markers, and each has a limited size. Camping is also permitted at other points around the lake, but the camper must be at least 150 ft. (46 m) back from the shore. No camping is allowed in or near any buildings.

At the present time, recreational opportunities are best for the canoeist. Day trips inland are possible, however. From the parking area gate, the hiker can walk along the dirt road 1.5 mi. (2.4 km) to the lake shore. Still farther along this road, at 3.2 mi. (5.2 km), the site of the former Nehasane Lodge is reached.

Mt. Frederica (sometimes called Smith's Summit or Summit Rock) rises 500 ft. (153 m) above Lake Lila. Mount Frederica is inland a bit, but also is frequently climbed.

The experienced outdoorsperson or backwoods skier can travel to Niger Lake (Negro Lake on older maps) by swinging northwest, where Forest Preserve land leads into the Five Ponds Wilderness Area. Pigeon Lake Wilderness Area is to the west. The expert backpacker can bushwhack through this country, but it is definitely not advised for the novice since there are few, if any, trails here. Because a lot of the land is privately owned and the trails indicated on the dated maps are undependable, anyone contemplating going into this region should plan his or her trip very carefully.

Index

INDEX OF PEOPLE

About the Author

Bruce Wadsworth is a retired science educator in Lake Placid, New York. He holds degrees from Alfred University, Syracuse University and the State University at Albany. He has participated in National Science Foundation Institutes in geology of North America at Vassar and in cytology and bio-chemistry at Alfred University. In addition, he took part in in-depth studies of Adirondack biosystems at the Cranberry Lake Biological Station, SUNY College of Environmental Science and Forestry.

His family of four became "46ers" after climbing each of the High Peaks together, and Wadsworth has been an end-to-ender on the Northville–Placid Trail four times. Early spring usually finds him clearing hiking trails. Special interests include wilderness preservation and Adirondack history. He is an active member of the Adirondack Mountain Club (ADK) and the author of several ADK publications.

Working for wilderness and loving it.

JOIN US!

We are a nonprofit membership organization that brings together people with interests in recreation, conservation, and environmental education in the New York State Forest Preserve. Our 23,000 members pursue a wide range of outdoor activities, including hiking, canoeing, backpacking, climbing, skiing, and snowshoeing. Many also join ADK to support our work on trails and in the halls of government, and thus lend their voices to protecting New York's Adirondack and Catskill parks.

Other benefits include:
- receipt of *Adirondac* seven times per year
- discounts on ADK publications, educational workshops, and wilderness lodges
- the opportunity to join a local chapter and enjoy its outings and activities
- the opportunity to apply for the ADK Visa card

BACKCOUNTRY EDUCATION & STEWARDSHIP

ADK is a leader in teaching outdoor skills and promoting recreational activities consistent with the region's wild character. Thus the Club offers workshops ranging from field natural history to hiking, canoeing, and skiing, and orienteering and wilderness first aid.

In addition, ADKers are known for "giving back" to the places that have nurtured them, by participating in extensive work on trails throughout the New York State Forest Preserve.

For more information about the Adirondacks or about ADK:
Information Center & Headquarters
814 Goggins Road, Lake George, NY 12845-4117
518 / 668-4447
Exit 21 off I-87 ("the Northway"), 9N south

May–Columbus Day:	Tues. after Columbus Day–May:
Mon.–Sat., 8:30 a.m.–5 p.m.	Mon.-Fri., 8:30 a.m.–4:30 p.m.

For lodge, cabin, or campground reservations on ADK's Heart Lake property in the High Peaks region, write or call:
Adirondack Mountain Club
Box 867
Lake Placid, NY 12946-0867
518/523-3441
(9 a.m.–7 p.m. daily)

To join ADK by credit card from within the U.S., please call our toll-free number: 800-395-8080 (8:30 a.m.–4:30 p.m., M–F). Callers who join may take immediate discount on ADK publications, workshops, and lodge stays and may charge all to VISA, MasterCard, Discover or American Express.

✂- -

Membership

Adirondack ADK Mountain Club

To Join:

Call **1-800-395-8080** or send this form with payment to
Adirondack Mountain Club
814 Goggins Road
Lake George, NY 12845-4117

Check Membership Level:

☐ Patron	$125*
☐ Supporting	$75*
☐ Family	$45*
☐ Adult	$40
☐ Senior Family	$35*
☐ Senior (65+)	$30
☐ Junior (under 18)	$25
☐ Student (18+, full time)	$25

School _____

Includes associate/family members
All fees subject to change.

Name _____
Address _____
City _____ State _____ Zip _____
Home Telephone (___) _____

☐ I want to join as a member-at-large.
☐ I want to join as a _____ Chapter member.
List spouse & children under 18 with birthdates:
Spouse _____
Child _____ Birthdate _____
Child _____ Birthdate _____
Bill my: ☐ Visa ☐ M/C ☐ Discover ☐ AmEx Exp. date _____

_____
Signature (required for charge)

ADK is a nonprofit, tax-exempt organization. Membership fees are tax deductible, as allowed by law. Please allow 6-8 weeks for receipt of first issue of **Adirondac**.

AS2

The Adirondack Mountain Club, Inc.
814 Goggins Road
Lake George, N.Y. 12845-4117
(518) 668-4447 / To order: 800-395-8080 (8:30–5:00, M–F)

BOOKS

85 Acres: A Field Guide to the Adirondack Alpine Summits

Adirondack Canoe Waters: North Flow

Adirondack Canoe Waters: South & West Flow

The Adirondack Mountain Club Canoe Guide to
Western & Central New York State

Adirondack Park Mountain Bike Preliminary
Trail and Route Listing

The Adirondack Reader

Adirondack Wildguide

An Adirondack Sampler: Day Hikes for All Seasons

Classic Adirondack Ski Tours

Climbing in the Adirondacks: A Guide to Rock & Ice Routes

Forests & Trees of the Adirondack High Peaks Region

Guide to Adirondack Trails: High Peaks Region

Guide to Adirondack Trails: Northern Region

Guide to Adirondack Trails: Central Region

Guide to Adirondack Trails: Northville–Placid Trail

Guide to Adirondack Trails: West-Central Region

Guide to Adirondack Trails: Eastern Region

Guide to Adirondack Trails: Southern Region

Guide to Catskill Trails

Kids on the Trail! Hiking with Children in the Adirondacks

Our Wilderness: How the People of New York Found,
Changed, and Preserved the Adirondacks

Trailside Notes: A Naturalist's Companion to Adirondack Plants

With Wilderness at Heart: A Short History of the
Adirondack Mountain Club

Winterwise: A Backpacker's Guide

MAPS

Trails of the Adirondack High Peaks Region

Trails of the Northern Region

Trails of the Central Region

Northville-Placid Trail

Trails of the West-Central Region

Trails of the Eastern Region

Trails of the Southern Region

Price list available on request.